323.44 FLI

Freedom

D1342229

KEY CONCEPTS

Published

Barbara Adam, Time
Alan Aldridge, Consumption
Alan Aldridge, The Market
Colin Barnes and Geoff Mercer, Disability
Darin Barney, The Network Society
Mildred Blaxter, Health
Harriet Bradley, Gender
Harry Brighouse, Justice
Steve Bruce, Fundamentalism
Margaret Canovan, The People
Alejandro Colás, Empire
Anthony Elliott, Concepts of the Self
Steve Fenton, Ethnicity
Michael Freeman, Human Rights
Russell Hardin, Trust
Fred Inglis, Culture
Jennifer Jackson Preece, Minority Rights
Paul Kelly, Liberalism
Anne Mette Kjær, Governance
Ruth Lister, Poverty
John Mandle, Global Justice
Michael Saward, Democracy
John Scott, Power
Anthony D. Smith, Nationalism
Stuart White, Equality

Freedom

Contemporary Liberal Perspectives

Katrin Flikschuh

polity

The right of Katrin Flikschuh to be identified as Author of this Work has been asserted in accordance with the UK Copyright, Designs and Patents Act 1988.

First published in 2007 by Polity Press

Polity Press
65 Bridge Street
Cambridge CB2 1UR, UK

Polity Press
350 Main Street
Malden, MA 02148, USA

ISBN-13: 978-07456-2437-2
ISBN-13: 978-07456-2438-9 (pb)

A catalogue record for this book is available from the British Library.

Typeset in 10.5 on 12 pt Sabon
by Servis Filmsetting Ltd, Manchester
Printed and bound in India by Replika Press PVT Ltd,

The publisher has used its best endeavours to ensure that the URLs for external websites referred to in this book are correct and active at the time of going to press. However, the publisher has no responsibility for the websites and can make no guarantee that a site will remain live or that the content is or will remain appropriate.

Every effort has been made to trace all copyright holders, but if any have been inadvertently overlooked the publishers will be pleased to include any necessary credits in any subsequent reprint or edition.

For further information on Polity, visit our website: www.polity.co.uk

Contents

To Bob Goodin,
whose fault it all is . . .

Acknowledgements

Apart from my undergraduate students at Essex and particularly my graduate students at the LSE, I would like to thank Janet Coleman, Stephen Houlgate, Paul Kelly, Christian List, Mike Otsuka, Tom Sorell and Leif Wenar, for their contributions, wittingly or otherwise, at various stages in the writing of this book. Many thanks are due to Emma Hutchinson and Louise Knight at Polity Press for their initial patience, later nudgings, and impressive efficiency at crucial stages. My warmest thanks to Diarmuid Costello – fellow academic, householder, and sleep-deprived parent – for *excellent* argument throughout: if not about freedom, then about the domestic constraints surrounding the writing of a book on it! My longest-standing debt is to Bob Goodin, my former undergraduate tutor, whose ferociously unforgiving course on 'Liberal Principles and Public Policy' first set me on the way, and whose unwavering support has helped sustain me on the road ever since.

Introduction: Approaching Liberal Freedom

I. The Scope of this Book

This book offers an introduction to the idea of freedom. Its target audience are second- and third-year undergraduate students in political philosophy and political theory – though there is always the hope that individual chapters may also be of interest to those further up the academic scale. As an introduction to the topic, this book is in many ways incomplete. In part, it is incomplete in that it considers only the *liberal* idea of freedom: socialist, Marxist, republican approaches do not get a look-in. Nor does this book touch upon ancient and other pre-modern freedom traditions. Such narrowness in scope may seem odd: is it worth writing a whole book just on liberal freedom? The answer is 'yes': indeed, one book is far from enough! I cover no more than a small chunk of the fascinating freedom debate in the history of liberal political thought – no more than the last fifty years: in truth, the focus is on the last thirty years.

One reason for this restriction in scope is space: one cannot reasonably hope to cover everything in a book this size. Another is competence: if I did know much about Marxist freedom, or about the ancient tradition, I might have written about them. However, I am not trained to do so, and I believe that it is not encouraging when, in writing an introductory book, one finds oneself going off to read up on the material.

Introductory books should be written on the basis of a certain amount of accumulated inside understanding. To the degree that I have any of that, I have it in contemporary liberal political philosophy. A third reason is relevance. I do not mean that studying Marxism or the Ancients is irrelevant: far from it. Oddly, though, there seem to be more general introductions to political theory and political philosophy thematizing Marxism and Marxist conceptions of freedom than there are accessible books about liberal freedom, in particular, *contemporary* liberal freedom. It may seem as though, whilst people think that Marxist freedom is worth studying because now somewhat quixotic, liberal freedom is too close to home, too familiar to bother with. Perhaps this is part of the explanation; however, my sense is that the current neglect is a consequence more of contemporary liberalism's own somewhat skewed preoccupations.

II. Its Structure

When Polity initially approached me about writing an introductory book on freedom I was teaching a second- and third-year core course in contemporary political philosophy at the University of Essex. The course was structured around John Rawls's *A Theory of Justice*. We did look at other contemporary political thinkers as well, but we tended to treat their work as responses to Rawls. And given Rawls's own focus on liberal justice, the course likewise focused on justice, sidelining other important liberal ideas and principles. I do not think I was the only convenor of an undergraduate course in political philosophy who found herself exposing her students to a systematically structured diet of Rawls and his respondents. I suspect that versions of my course are replicated year in, year out, up and down the country. There is eminently good reason for this: given the immense importance of his work, no undergraduate political philosophy or politics student can afford to walk away with a degree one of the components of which does not include a fairly systematic exposure, at some point, to Rawls. The resulting neglect of other eminent contemporary authors and liberal ideas is nonetheless regrettable. So when the idea of a freedom book was mooted, my first thought was 'Well, it's not going to be on Rawls!'

Admittedly, my second thought was that it would be desirable for the proposed book to be broadly continuous with Rawls's legacy – that it should not stand apart, like an albatross, from what I conjectured to be the core curriculum concerns of most political philosophy or theory courses in the English-speaking world. I wanted to write a book on the liberal idea of freedom which, whilst it did not take Rawls as its point of departure, nonetheless focused on the contemporary debate. The initial decision to *exclude* Rawls led me to think about whom to *include* instead: it led me to favour an author-focused approach over a topic-centred one. Once I had put Rawls to one side, I returned to my various course reading lists, scanning them for alternative philosophical eminences. It quickly became apparent that if I was going to write about contemporary liberal freedom, one thinker I would have to engage with was Hillel Steiner, whose work contains one of the most innovative developments of the subject. But if I included Steiner, I would also need to count in Robert Nozick, who crucially inspired Steiner's work. That left me with two libertarian thinkers – one extravagantly left-leaning, the other more classically to the right. I needed some counterweights. One obvious candidate was Ronald Dworkin, whose liberal egalitarian outlook could help make up, to some extent, for the exclusion of Rawls. But having paired Steiner with Nozick, who should I pair Dworkin with? I considered Amartya Sen, whose developmental perspective on freedom takes him interestingly beyond the conceptual confines of Western liberal societies. However, Tom Sorell rightly impressed upon me the indispensability of including Joseph Raz in any book on contemporary conceptions of liberal freedom: so I ended up replacing Sen's capabilities approach with Raz's liberal perfectionism.

The general structure of the last two-thirds of the book thus emerged relatively quickly from the decision to examine the work of some of Rawls's most prominent contemporaries rather than that of Rawls himself. At some point whilst pairing Nozick with Steiner and Dworkin with Raz I ceased thinking in terms of my initial libertarian / egalitarian distinction: given the substitution of Raz for Sen, I had little choice.

Yet I doggedly continued to think in pairwise terms, and gradually the negative / positive distinction began to strike me as the most salient in the recent history of liberal freedom. I began to think of Nozick and Steiner as proponents of divergent conceptions of negative freedom, and of Dworkin and Raz as advocates of differing conceptions of positive freedom (that the reading of Dworkin in positive terms is somewhat contentious struck me only much later, but I like to think that I make a reasonably good case for it in chapter 5). Introducing the negative / positive distinction brought me to Isaiah Berlin, to whom that distinction is due: and if Berlin was in, Gerald MacCallum would have to be, too, since his contribution to the debate did most to cast doubt on the cogency of Berlin's distinction. This, finally, settled the overall structure of the book: it would broadly chart the fate within contemporary liberal freedom debates of Berlin's seminal distinction between negative and positive freedom traditions, asking, among other things, how that distinction continues to be employed and interpreted in the face of MacCallum's influential critique of its philosophical coherence.

III. Method

Despite his generally acknowledged intellectual eminence, Isaiah Berlin does not have a high profile among contemporary liberal philosophers. Many tend to turn a little high-minded at the mention of his name: 'not really a philosopher', one hears, 'more a historian of ideas' (as though the latter was something to feel self-conscious about). I wasn't initially very happy about the inclusion of Berlin either: I never much liked the things he had to say about what he calls the positive freedom tradition and, in that context, his appraisal of Kant in particular. But if one is going to structure an author-focused freedom book along the negative / positive axis, there is simply no way around Berlin.

Including Berlin turned out to be an excellent decision, not least methodologically. Among the principal explanations for Berlin's current lack for profile in academic philosophy is the abiding underlying influence of the method of conceptual analysis, which rose to prominence during the 1950s, repudiating 'grand theorizing' in favour of 'modest analysis', therewith eclipsing Berlin's own more eclectic and synthetic style of thinking (I shall say more about the method of conceptual analysis in chapter 2). This new way of doing philosophy had little patience with Berlin's sweeping historical statements – including his negative / positive distinction – which it found non-rigorous, overly general, and lacking in 'logical truth'. Yet, tellingly, 'grand theorizing' was declared rejuvenated upon Rawls's publication of *A Theory of Justice*: and indeed, and although much more rigorous in the now requisite sense, Rawls is also, like Berlin, a synthetic thinker given to making large, imprecise, and wholly original statements. One difference between Berlin and Rawls in this respect is that Rawls's sweeping statements tend to be internal to his liberal theory of justice; Berlin's grand claims, by contrast, range over the whole history of liberal political thought. Yet, given the partial overlap in general philosophical temperament between them, Berlin provided an unexpected degree of continuity with the more synthetic style of philosophical argumentation reintroduced by Rawls and also pursued by the four thinkers here considered.

Of course, Nozick, Steiner, Dworkin and Raz are all thinkers squarely in the analytic tradition of Anglo-American philosophy: they are all conceptual analysts at one level of argumentation. But the theorizing of none of them is reducible to this method. To the contrary, the reputation of each is based on the idiosyncrasy and originality of their developed philosophical positions, and on their ability to theorize liberal freedom in the context of more general concerns of liberal political morality. It is among the aims of the present book to communicate a sense of the diversity and vitality of the contemporary freedom debate by situating individual thinkers' freedom positions within their broader philosophical and political commitments, including not only their respective theories of distributive justice, but also their intellectual debts to their various historical predecessors. A concern running across the remit of the individual chapters is to draw attention to the enormously important philosophical *history* of liberal freedom without which current liberal thinking could not proceed in the way in which it does. Again, it is Berlin who understood this better than others, and again Rawls seems to me to have reintroduced some appreciation of the history of political thought into contemporary political philosophy. Hobbes, Locke, Hume, Kant and Mill are the thinkers who have given our understanding of liberalism its current form; it is not possible to gain an adequate insight into current freedom debates without some appreciation of the crucial contributions of these historical figures.

Here, a certain difficulty had to be confronted. It is not feasible to set out Hobbes's views on freedom, say, without taking for granted quite a lot about Hobbes's general philosophical and political position. The way in which historical thinkers are referred to in this book can be demanding for readers who have had no prior exposure to Mill, Hume and Kant. There will be times when I refer to Kant's conception of 'external freedom', for example, and when relevantly uninitiated readers may simply draw a blank. Most of the time, I will have said enough to give beginners a reasonably good sense of what non-interference means in Hobbes, freedom of choice in Hume, self-development in Mill: but since it is not possible for me to offer a comprehensive introduction to all of them, I decided to avoid oversimplification even at the risk of stretching the patience of some of the book's principal addressees. If this does happen, readers should take comfort from the fact that simplification is not, in any case, a good idea. The things one first reads about a historical thinker tend to stick with one: better, therefore, to gain an initial impression of great sophistication and complexity than to come away with the view that someone like Hobbes can be adequately summed up in a couple of pages of an introductory book. My hope is that readers will take any difficulties they might encounter on this score in the spirit of awakened curiosity – that they will be inspired to consult further texts: even the works of these thinkers themselves. To this end I have provided some guidance to further introductory reading in relevant notes.

There is yet another aspect of Berlin's general style of approach which chimes in this time with my own philosophical predilections rather than those of Rawls. I refer to Berlin's appreciation of the ways in which any particular conception of political freedom – freedom of choice and action – is implicated metaphysically. Metaphysics is a topic liable to studied silence amongst contemporary liberal philosophers. Rawls himself counsels a strategy of avoidance, and most have followed his counsel. Of course, suspicion towards metaphysics is nothing new in the Anglo-American philosophical tradition, going back at least to Hume and even to Hobbes. In relation to liberal freedom debates, the current orthodoxy asserts that one can perfectly thoroughly discuss the politics of freedom without ever needing to allude to the metaphysics of free will. I have never found claims of this sort persuasive; it has always seemed to me that those who make them in fact occupy metaphysical positions falling under the umbrella of what is known as 'compatibilism'. I was thus surprised and relieved, upon rereading Berlin's 'Two Concepts of Liberty' and related essays, to note his unmistakably incompatibilist sentiments breaking through again and again in the course of his writings on the history and politics of liberal freedom. In contrast to the implicitly compatibilist tone of much current liberal theorizing, Berlin unapologetically embraces a version of incompatibilism – albeit not one he develops systematically.

Taking its cue from Berlin (and my own predilections), this book also tries to chart the relationship between individual thinkers' accounts of political freedom – freedom of choice and action – and their underlying metaphysical free will commitments. I argue that one cannot fully understand Nozick's defence of individual freedom of choice unless one takes into account his incompatibilist position on free will; nor can one easily make sense of Dworkin's insistence upon individual responsibility for choice unless one appreciates his compatibilist conception of personal development and character building. That said, the metaphysics here employed is low-level: all the reader really needs to be aware of to begin with is the broad compatibilist / incompatibilist distinction.[1]

Compatibilists are so called because they believe the idea of free will to be compatible with the thesis of determinism. According to the thesis of determinism, everything in nature, including human choice and action, is subject to the laws of causality. This thesis may seem to rule out the possibility of free will in the intuitively strong sense of the will as constituting a capacity for 'uncaused' willing and choosing. However, compatibilists reject as metaphysically extravagant the idea of freedom as requiring some mysterious *uncaused* spontaneity of the will. According to compatibilists, *given* thoroughgoing causal determination, our freedom explanations must fit into the general causal framework to be coherent. Free will is therefore interpreted as denoting no more than externally unconstrained willing. Relatedly, free choice is interpreted as unconstrained choice between two or more available options. On this view, the will is free so long as no external impediments – such as the will of another – prevent it from exercising choice with regard to two or more available options. However, the will is not free in some deep, metaphysically mysterious sense of being 'unbound' by the causality of nature. Crucially, the will could not choose not to choose when presented with options: for compatibilists, there is no 'freedom of indifference', as Hume referred to the idea of uncaused free choice (I shall say more about Hume's position on this in chapters 1, 2 and 5).

Incompatibilists deny the compatibility of free will and thoroughgoing determinism. Sometimes this denial takes the form of rejecting either the determinism thesis or the idea of free will: on this version of incompatibilism, we can have either determinism or freedom, but not both. Most of those who find themselves confronted with this choice tend to choose determinism over freedom. A different kind of incompatibilism argues that determinism and freedom are both possible, but that they operate at different levels of human experience. These incompatibilists commit themselves to showing that there is a sense in which the human will can be thought of as non-determined causally, even granting the applicability of the thesis of determinism to the rest of nature. Unsurprisingly, this is very difficult to do. Incompatibilists' strategy is often to contest, as a first step, the plausibility of compatibilist accounts of freedom at the level of *moral* experience. If all human actions and choices are ultimately caused, incompatibilists contend, no one can ever be held responsible for their actions. In that case compatibilists can make no sense of a domain of human experience – moral responsibility and moral culpability – which we regard as absolutely central to our self-understanding as agents.[2] For these incompatibilists, defending the possibility of uncaused free will even in the face of acceptance of determinism with regard to the rest of nature may be a Herculean task; yet the alternative – compromising on the demands of morality – is even more unpalatable. In the end, therefore, incompatibilists bite the bullet metaphysically, committing themselves to a view of the human will as categorically distinct, in some sense, from the rest of nature. This is deemed 'high metaphysics' – i.e. a metaphysics that posits some sort of distinction between nature and non-nature: a risky position to occupy in the modern scientific world, though much depends on how precisely one interprets this notion of the 'non-natural'.

There are many different positions within compatibilism and incompatibilism respectively. These are sometimes classified into soft and hard compatibilisms / incompatibilisms; there is also a position that characterizes itself as noncompatibilist in distinction from both of the two dominant theories. None of these finer distinctions will concern us in the following chapters. For our purposes it is enough to keep in mind that compatibilists believe free will and free choice to be explicable within the framework of causal determination, whereas incompatibilists deny this. We shall see that the classic statement of compatibilism is associated with Hume, and a (complicated) version of incompatibilism with Kant, and we shall examine the explicit and implicit influence of these historical metaphysicians upon the work of contemporary authors.

IV. Themes

I have said that this book is written in the synthetic style, by which I mean that each chapter includes, apart from an analytic component, an interest in each thinker's overall political position, an examination of the trajectory of his historical intellectual debts, and a concern to draw out his explicit or implicit metaphysical free will commitments. Most of the themes of the book have thus already been mentioned in the course of setting out its method.

Is there an overall 'grand' theme, though? Not really. I initially expected there to be at least one major theme, but things did not turn out that way. This happens often enough: one goes where the argument takes one. Still, my one intended major theme was to argue the indispensability of *some* acknowledged connection between freedom and reason. This is a Kantian theme, of course, so not surprising for a Kantian such as myself to alight upon. My intention was to resuscitate that aspect of the positive concept of freedom which Berlin is so scathing about. The plan was to evaluate each individual freedom contribution in the light of the space it gives over to that elusive freedom / reason connection – to the thought, that is, of there being a fairly intimate relationship between our status as reasoning beings and our thinking ourselves free. It has always seemed to me that the moral significance of our freedom is non-divorceable from our reasoning capacities, and that acknowledgement of this non-separability entails acknowledgement of certain freedom *responsibilities* – not just freedom *claims*. This idea of human freedom as explicable, ultimately, only in terms of our moral responsibilities is in many respects quite non-individualistic. As I suggest towards the end of chapter 1, its non-individualism may be one of the principal reasons for Berlin's overall rejection of Kantian freedom and the positive tradition associated with it. My personal quest in relation to this book was to restore this Kantian dimension to greater prominence within the contemporary liberal freedom debate.

However, things did not work out that way. Of the thinkers here examined, only Joseph Raz draws an explicit connection between freedom and reason: but he does so from an Aristotelian perspective, which lies in many ways beyond the remit of the negative / positive distinction as drawn by Berlin. There is a hint of a connection in Nozick's decisionistic free will analysis, and there is also, I argue in chapter 4, an implicit reliance by Steiner upon reasoning beings' capacity for moral obligation – however much disavowed by Steiner himself in his rigorously descriptive approach. Overall, though, the relationship between freedom and reason is given little systematic treatment in current liberal freedom debates. This is itself an interesting result, though not one I set out to arrive at.

The overall theme, such as it is, which emerged instead is that there isn't really one single criterion or even set of criteria by which we can gauge and evaluate, let alone rank, the liberal freedom conceptions here examined. Instead, there is diversity, though, oddly, no resulting incoherence. Liberal thinkers do disagree about the meaning and significance of freedom, often quite radically so. Despite this, one does not gain the impression that they are simply talking past one another, or that they cannot fathom the source of their disagreements and what hangs on them politically. A Rawlsian might be tempted to say that the reason why there is diversity without incoherence is that the disagreements are reasonable ones: there is enough of an overlapping consensus on the meaning of liberal freedom to sustain divergences at the edges, as it were. But I don't think that quite captures it. My own sense is that freedom is a metaphysically, and hence normatively, indeterminate idea – one the full grasp of which constitutively eludes us. It seems to me that the fact that this metaphysically, and normatively indeterminate ideal lies at the heart of liberal political thinking does much to account for liberalism's continued vitality even today – including the (ambivalent) fascination which liberalism exerts even upon many non-liberals. This, at any rate, is the major conclusion I myself drew in the course of writing this book – that we should not look for philosophical unanimity where none is to be had; that we should enjoy, instead, the diversity of liberal freedom meanings and commitments. Obviously, this does not debar those who read this book from drawing different conclusions about the arguments and positions here examined.

1

Isaiah Berlin: *Two* Concepts of Liberty?

I. Introduction

Isaiah Berlin's 'Two Concepts of Liberty' was first delivered in the form of a public lecture in 1958, when the Cold War was well under way.[1] The essay has since been published in many different editions of Berlin's considerable volume of work on (the history of) liberal thought. What is the abiding significance of 'Two Concepts' nearly fifty years on? Responses to this question will vary depending on whom one asks. Those who take umbrage at the unmistakably ideological undertones of Berlin's essay will be inclined to say that the essay's influence on the philosophical study of freedom has been inflated.[2] Others – often those who knew him as colleague or teacher – will insist that without Berlin our understanding of liberal freedom would not be what it is today.[3] From the perspective of contemporary analytic political philosophy, the significance of Berlin's essay is often thought to lie in the fact that the contestation over 'Two Concepts' gave rise, eventually, to the now perhaps equally widely accepted understanding of freedom as a 'triadic' concept within those circles. This is Gerald MacCallum's contention, to be examined in the next chapter, that there is only *one* concept of liberty – albeit one that contains both 'negative' and 'positive' elements within it.[4]

From this last-mentioned perspective, the significance of Berlin's essay is that it provided the opportunity for much-needed philosophical analysis and clarification of the concept of liberty, or freedom.[5] This may be one way of saying that Berlin's essay lacks the clarity and rigour demanded by current analytic philosophy. Others – often those working in the history of ideas – complain that the essay lacks a scholar's differentiated understanding of particular philosophical thinkers in the history of ideas, that it ignores necessary attention to interpretative detail. Both charges have some warrant: not only does Berlin speak, without any sense of incoherence, of there being two distinct *concepts* of liberty – he also offers a flamboyantly idiosyncratic reading of the history of ideas that makes Rousseau and Hegel, and at times even Mill and Locke, political bedfellows of a Lenin or a Stalin. From whichever perspective or discipline one comes at it, 'Two Concepts' provokes controversy.

That said, the negative / positive distinction has a way of rearing its head in discussions about freedom even above conceptual analysts' insistent declarations of triadic unity. It is a powerful distinction, and Berlin's discussion of it, too, is powerful, despite its lack of analytic rigour, despite its seemingly wilful historical distortions, despite its irritating ideological undertones. What, precisely, is so powerful about Berlin's discussion is difficult to say. For the purposes of the present chapter I shall take the essay's principal importance to be twofold: first, Berlin's identification of two conflicting traditions of specifically *liberal* thinking on freedom, and second, his implicit appreciation of the disparate metaphysical commitments that thinkers invariably bring to bear in articulating and evaluating the idea of freedom. The first of these two themes in Berlin's essay has received a lot of attention. The thought is surely arresting that the liberal tradition, which one expects, like any tradition, to display a fair degree of internal cohesiveness, should find itself in such sharp internal conflict with regard to an idea that is central to it. Minor differences or disagreements about this or that principle or value at the periphery of the tradition are one thing: but that the liberal view should come apart so fundamentally with regard to what lies at the core of its value system is rather remarkable. Identifying and thematizing this remarkable fact about the liberal tradition is no small thing.[6]

The second theme has received much less attention. At any rate, it has been given more oblique treatment, partly in the form of discussions of the problem of the 'contented slave' – a topic to which I shall return below. There are two principal reasons for the relative neglect of this second aspect – the divergent metaphysical presuppositions underlying conflicting normative interpretations of the liberal idea of freedom. The first is that Berlin's explicit references to the metaphysics of freedom in 'Two Concepts' take a critical expression: he is chiefly concerned to expose and to reject the metaphysics he detects as underlying the concept of positive freedom. In 'Two Concepts' Berlin's own metaphysical commitments take a back seat: their background presence in that essay must be extrapolated on the basis of related essays, such as 'Historical Inevitability', 'From Hope and Fear Set Free', and other writings.[7] The second reason for neglect has to do with the general attitude of suspicion towards issues in metaphysics among contemporary political philosophers. It is now generally assumed to be perfectly possible to inquire into 'freedom of action' – that aspect of the idea of freedom directly relevant to politics – without assuming any position at all on the metaphysics of 'free will'. In order to specify under what conditions and to what extent persons can be said to be free to engage in activities unhindered by others, we need not settle the question as to whether these persons have free will – whether they are free in the intuitively appealing but philosophically problematic sense of possessing a will not determined by laws of natural causality.

As it happens, most of those who believe that one can coherently talk about freedom of action without touching upon the issue of free will are compatibilists, who reject the idea of free will in any strong, non-determinist sense and who embrace instead a certain conception of free choice which they deem to be perfectly compatible with the determinism of natural causality. Berlin's position on this issue is unusual. Berlin's antipathies towards the metaphysics of *reason*, which he rightly associates with the positive tradition, might lead one to expect him to be sympathetic to compatibilism. In fact, however, Berlin has robustly incompatibilist sympathies – in relation to human agency, he believes suspension of the thesis of determinism to be necessary if the idea of freedom is to have any moral significance for us: 'The central assumption of common human thought and speech seems to me to be that freedom is the principal characteristic that distinguishes man from all that is non-human.'[8] While Berlin concedes that this 'central assumption' constitutes no disproof of the thesis of determinism, he nonetheless insists that, were humans seriously to submit to that thesis within the sphere of practical agency, neither the language of moral responsibility nor that of individual choice could have the normative significance we assign them.[9] As we shall see below, these incompatibilist sentiments of free will which are largely *implicit* in 'Two Concepts' complicate Berlin's reasons for rejecting the metaphysics of positive freedom.

The greater part of the present chapter will be concerned with explicating Berlin's distinction between negative and positive freedom with a view towards assessing its continuing relevance for current liberal freedom disputes. An explication of Berlin's distinction does, however, throw up the question as to its sustainability – substantively as well as conceptually.[10] Can the negative / positive distinction be upheld, or must it finally collapse? The question as to the conceptual sustainability of the distinction forms the theme of the next chapter. The question of its substantive sustainability arises in the context of the problem of the contented slave and constitutes the subject matter of discussion in the second half of the present chapter. More specifically, it is the problem of the contented slave which raises the question as to whether the negative concept of freedom can get by entirely without appeal to a connection between freedom and reason of the kind that Berlin attributes to the positive concept of freedom. It is in this context that Berlin's metaphysical commitments are of interest. I shall begin in section II with a discussion of the negative / positive distinction as conceived by Berlin. In section III I shall then introduce the problem of the contented slave, showing how it challenges the substantive sustainability of that distinction. Finally, section IV considers the relevance of Berlin's incompatibilist sentiments to his response to the problem of the contented slave.

II. Berlin's Negative / Positive Distinction

What is negative about negative freedom, what positive about positive freedom? As I have said, what is interesting about

Berlin's distinction in 'Two Concepts' is that he thinks of the negative and the positive freedom concepts as having evolved within the *liberal* tradition of political thought. Given this, Berlin's distinction between negative and positive freedom should not be immediately equated with Benjamin Constant's earlier differentiation between 'the liberty of the moderns' and the 'liberty of the ancients'. For Constant, the liberty of the moderns marks the triumph of individualistic commercial society over the pre-modern non-individualistic understanding of a socio-political community as an organic unit. Moderns associate individual freedom with the absence of constraints, including the constraints of law, to pursue one's own interests – especially those of a commercial kind. Constant contrasts this with the ancient Greco-Roman understanding of liberty in terms of being a freeman as opposed to a slave and of being entitled, indeed obliged, to take an active role in government.

Berlin's view of negative liberty substantially overlaps with Constant's 'liberty of the moderns'. In his initial sketch of the basic difference between *his* 'two senses of liberty' Berlin says that proponents of negative liberty ask, 'What is the area within which the subject – a person or group of persons – is or should be left to do or be what he is able to do or be, without interference by other persons?'[11] The catchword here is non-interference, and although Berlin speaks loosely of non-interference *by others*, whereas Constant emphasizes non-interference by *government*, it is clear that Berlin is as much concerned with governmental as with individual non-interference with a person's capacity to do or be what they want to do or be.

By contrast, proponents of positive freedom ask, 'What, or who, is the source of control or interference that can determine someone to do, or be, this rather than that?'[12] In contrast to Berlin's summary statement of negative freedom, the relevant catchword in what he says about positive freedom is more difficult to identify. This encourages the supposition that, in so far as what Berlin says about negative freedom sounds more or less like what Constant says about the liberty of the moderns, what Berlin says about positive freedom is probably also much like what his predecessor meant by the liberty of the ancients. Yet Berlin's placement of the concept of positive freedom within the liberal tradition should caution against this move. It is a distinctive feature of the liberal tradition that it takes the individual person to be the basic unit of moral and political analysis and concern. This was not so for the ancients, for whom the individual was a constituent part of the *polis* as *their* basic unit of analysis. To be a freeman rather than a slave was to be a citizen, and a citizen's role was to take an active part in governing the *polis*. By contrast, Berlin's gloss on the liberal concept of positive freedom asks what or who is the source of control of the *individual person*, and his answer is that, according to proponents of positive freedom, the source of such control should be each person him or herself. Thus, whereas for the ancients to be free was to participate in governing the *polis*, for a proponent of liberal positive freedom, as Berlin understands it, to be free is to govern *oneself*. As with the concept of negative freedom, so the concept of positive freedom takes the individual person as its basic unit of analysis. It is this feature of Berlin's 'two senses of liberty' that makes both distinctly *liberal* ideas of freedom. The difference between them is that whilst the one associates freedom with the *absence* of constraint – hence *negative* freedom – the other associates it with the *presence* of (self-imposed) constraint – hence *positive* freedom.[13]

Like many others, Berlin finds the thought deeply counterintuitive, that the *presence* of constraint should form part of what it is to be free. He finds even the presence of *self-imposed* constraint counterintuitive in relation to freedom. And the idea of freedom as self-imposed constraint *is* problematic. If to be free is to impose a constraint upon oneself – if freedom is, in that sense, self-imposed, does one not have to be free to impose freedom upon oneself? Freedom as self-imposed constraint appears to presuppose the (self-determining) capacity to impose such constraint upon oneself. Some of Berlin's criticisms of positive freedom touch upon this philosophically problematic notion of freedom as self-imposed constraint. However, his principal worries are of a *political* nature. Berlin worries that the bifurcation within the metaphysics of positive freedom between the self as controller and the self as controlled makes that view vulnerable to political abuse. He has no such worries about the concept of negative freedom, which he finds both philosophically intuitive and politically robust.

II. 1. Berlin on negative freedom

Given his evident sympathies with it, Berlin's exposition of the concept of negative freedom is surprisingly short. This brevity may be a reflection of his convictions regarding the intuitive character of negative freedom: Berlin may think that not much *needs* to be said about negative freedom as a philosophical idea. 'Everything is what it is,' Berlin asserts; 'liberty is liberty, not equality, or fairness, or justice, or culture.'[14] So what *is* liberty? Berlin takes it to be a decisive advantage of the concept of negative liberty that it encapsulates exactly what liberty is, for, according to it, liberty is 'absence of external impediments'. According to Berlin, 'I am normally said to be free to the degree to which no man or body of men interferes with my activity. Political liberty in this sense is simply the area within which a man can act unobstructed by others.'[15] To be free is not to be interfered with by others.

The idea of freedom as non-interference is often associated with Hobbes.[16] Yet, according to Hobbes, many things other than persons can be free in the sense of not being subject to external impediments. Water hurtling down a stream is free so long as no barrier stops it in its flow. A boulder falling down a mountain is free until in hitting solid ground it is prevented from further descent. A man travelling along the road is free until stopped by a group of highwaymen who obstruct his way. According to Hobbes, objects as well as persons can be free. This is so principally because Hobbes thinks of persons as a type of object. Interestingly, even for Hobbes, mere non-interference appears not to be a *sufficient* condition of freedom. Water hurtling down a stream, a boulder falling off a mountain, a man travelling along the road, are each in a state of self-induced movement. The water's movement is caused by its current, that of the boulder by its own weight dragging it downwards, the man's by the inner desires which drive him on. Water in a still pond, a boulder wedged against the side of a mountain, a man asleep in his bed, would not, on Hobbes's account, be free. The reason for the unfreedom of these latter objects is not external interference but absence of self-induced movement. External interference can render unfree only things that were previously in a state of self-induced movement. External interference is a sufficient condition only of the *unfreedom* of objects that were previously in a state of (self-induced) freedom.

Berlin's view on negative freedom differs in some important respects from that of Hobbes. It resembles Hobbes's account in (over-)emphasizing the condition of non-interference even whilst presupposing that of self-induced movement or action. Berlin says, 'I am normally said to be free to the degree to which no man or body of men interferes with my activity.' The reference to 'my activity' indicates Berlin's implicit acknowledgement of self-induced movement as a necessary condition of freedom. Yet, only a page further on, Berlin says simply that 'by being free I mean not being interfered with by others'.[17] This second remark suggests that Berlin believes non-interference to be a necessary and sufficient condition of freedom. As will become evident below, Berlin's tendency to overlook the capacity for self-induced movement as a necessary condition of freedom, together with his focus on non-interference as a sufficient freedom condition, reveals something quite remarkable about his underlying metaphysics of freedom.

Although he shares Hobbes's emphasis on freedom as non-interference, Berlin's account is in other ways more restrictive than that of Hobbes. In particular, Berlin does not think that water or stones can be free. Only persons can be free. More controversially, Berlin also thinks that only other persons' interferences can render one unfree. Although he acknowledges that force of circumstance may prevent a person from carrying out their intended activity, he insists that such non-personal preventions do not render a person *unfree* to do what they want or intend to do. Berlin distinguishes between being unfree to do X and being unable to do X. According to him, the man who finds his path obstructed by a large boulder is not *unfree* to continue on his way but merely *unable* to do so. By contrast, the man who finds his path obstructed by highwaymen who threaten him is *unfree* to continue on his way.[18]

Berlin's departure from Hobbes's account in this respect is significant. The claim that only the interference of other persons can render one unfree is indicative of what Berlin takes to be the essence of freedom interference and what he takes to be the essence, therefore, of freedom itself. The essence of freedom interference is its coercive character. A boulder which in lying across the road prevents me from continuing on my way is not acting coercively towards me. By contrast, the highwaymen who prevent me from continuing along the road are acting coercively towards me. One might put it thus: the highwaymen know something about me which the boulder couldn't possibly know. They know of this aspect about me because they know of it in relation to themselves. They know that I have intentions – in this case, the intention of continuing down the road. They know that I have intentions because they know that they have intentions – in this case, to prevent me from continuing down the road. The specific prevention that amounts to an instance of unfreedom for Berlin is others' deliberate and successful frustration of another's pursuit of their intentions. But if being rendered unfree is, essentially, to have one's intentions coercively interfered with and altered, then only those beings can be free who are capable of having intentions. For Berlin, in contrast to Hobbes, only persons can be rendered unfree, because only persons have the capacity to form intentions that can be coercively interfered with by others. Clearly, for Berlin, persons are not simply one type of physical object.

It is a distinctive feature of the use of coercion that it need not include the use of physical force.[19] Someone may prevent me from continuing with my intended activity by forcing me physically to desist from this activity. The highwaymen might physically prevent me from walking down the road by tying me to a tree. Were they to do this, their prevention would in certain respects resemble the prevention caused by the boulder lying across the road. They would have rendered me physically unable to continue on my way. Typically, however, highwaymen do not need to resort to the use of physical force. Typically, their *threat* of the use of force is sufficient to make me do what they want me to do. It is the highwaymen's threat of the use of force that makes me stop in my tracks of my own accord. What is distinctive about coercion in contrast to physical force is the fact that its use is designed to have the effect of getting a person to change their intentions. In contrast to the use of physical prevention, the use of coercion works on a person's capacity to form and to change their intentions.

In that sense, coercion is directed at a person's will rather than their body.[20]

To sum up: according to Berlin, and in contrast to Hobbes, negative freedom specifies both a capacity of persons and a relation between persons. Only persons are capable of freedom, and only persons are capable of preventing others' freedom. Only persons are capable of freedom, because only persons are capable of forming and acting on intentions that are susceptible to freedom violations. In that sense the 'cause' of 'self-induced movement' is persons' capacity to form and to act on their intentions. In contrast to Hobbes, Berlin locates persons' capacity for freedom in a distinctive capacity of the will as the capacity to form and effect action on intentions. Hence, what is distinctive about freedom interferences is that they paradigmatically involve the use of coercion. Coercion is others' wilful interference with a person's given intentions with the aim of altering that person's intentions, thereby getting them to do something which they would not otherwise do. Since, for Berlin, only persons have power of intentional willing, only persons are capable of being coerced, and only persons are capable of coercing. Hence, only persons are capable of freedom, and only persons are capable of rendering others unfree.

Admittedly, little that Berlin says explicitly about negative freedom suggests this interpretation. As I said, most of the time Berlin focuses on the notion of non-interference with persons who are presumed already to be in a state of self-induced movement. But given Berlin's restriction of freedom attribution to persons, given his insistence upon coercion as the hallmark of freedom interferences, given the distinctive nature of coercion, which works upon the will, as opposed to force, which aims at physical prevention, the conclusion seems warranted that, for Berlin, freedom is not simply a state of non-prevented physical motion. To the contrary, the capacity for freedom has to do, for Berlin, with persons' capacity to form and pursue their own intentions. In that sense negative freedom is, for Berlin, a capacity of the will, and freedom preventions are interferences by others with a person's will. It is precisely this view of freedom prevention as interference with a person's *will* that fuels, I shall argue, Berlin's resistance to the concept of positive freedom.

II. 2. Berlin on positive freedom

I have not yet said anything about Berlin's position on governmental interference in relation to the concept of negative freedom. This may seem a strange omission, given Berlin's insistence upon negative freedom as a politically robust concept of liberty. For Berlin, a freedom-respecting government is simply a non-interfering government. Berlin acknowledged that governments, including liberal governments, pursue many objectives. Apart from preserving liberty, liberal governments pursue justice, for example, including social justice. Berlin further acknowledges that different liberal values and related government objectives may at times come into conflict – that these values and objectives cannot always all be satisfied at the same time. Even though he considers liberty to be an especially 'sacred value',[21] he concedes that liberal governments must sometimes sacrifice individual freedom for the sake of other values or objectives, such as the defence of national sovereignty, or the achievement of social justice. When liberal governments curtail individual freedom in these ways, they typically do so by coercive means. Berlin concedes that despite being a particularly sacred value, liberty is but one value among many. He accepts that governments' coercive interference with individuals' freedom can be legitimate so long as such interference is justified with reference to these other values.

An essential condition of governmental interference being justified is that governments acknowledge what they are doing. Recall Berlin's contention that, 'everything is what it is; liberty is liberty, not equality or fairness or justice or culture'.[22] As we have seen, Berlin's official position is that liberty is simply non-interference – though upon closer examination his actual position turns out to be more complex. Nonetheless, in so far as one takes one person's liberty to be a function of others' non-interference with that person, a government preserves liberty by not interfering. The less a government interferes, the more liberty persons have. Crucially, a government cannot preserve or increase liberty by any means other than non-interference. A government cannot increase individual liberty by means of securing greater social justice. To the contrary, when a government pursues social justice, it will typically end up curtailing individual liberty in its effort to achieve this particular objective. Berlin acknowledges that this may happen, and that it may happen justifiably. Yet when it does happen, a government should not try to persuade its citizens that the achievement of greater social justice amounts in itself to an increase in freedom.

One of Berlin's central objections to the concept of positive freedom is his claim that proponents of this view have a tendency to present freedom as something it isn't. Political usurpers of the concept of positive liberty are especially prone to persuading others that liberty is the achievement of equality, or justice, or that true liberty consists in dying for the sake of the revolution. Although Berlin concedes that such efforts constitute a political abuse of the concept of positive freedom, he also argues that there is something about the concept of positive freedom that lends itself to such abuse. This 'something' is a combination of two things: first, the metaphysical bifurcation of the person into a 'higher' and a 'lower' self, and second, an ideal of human perfectibility which assumes a strong connection between freedom, reason and truth.

Recall Berlin's initial sketch of positive freedom as asking, 'What, or who, is the source of control or interference that can determine someone to do, or be, this rather than that?'[23] I said that, on the positive account, freedom has something to do with the notion of self-imposed constraint, such that the free person is one who controls what they do or become. On the positive account, the source of control or interference with what a person does is the person him or herself. This idea of self-control implies the bifurcation of a person into controller and controlled, a bifurcation that is reflected in Berlin's claim that 'the "positive" sense of the word "liberty" derives from the wish on the part of the individual to be his own master'.[24] Talk of being one's own master has precisely this connotation of one part or aspect of oneself as being in control of some other part or aspect of oneself.

Why should this wish to be one's own master arise? Berlin thinks it arises from postulating the ideal of self-perfection. This ideal can be variously defined. However, it will usually involve a distinction between two states of being – an actual state and a possible state – where the latter is somehow seen as preferable to the former, and where the perception of the qualitative difference between them motivates the attempt to move from the actual state to the possible state. Berlin derives the positive sense of self-perfection from what he considers to be that tradition's more general fascination with rationality, or truth. Self-perfection is said to lie in the self's attainment of its 'true', 'higher' self. The self attains this state of perfection by abnegating or controlling its 'false', 'lower' self. Proponents of positive freedom divide the self into a higher and a lower self *because* they entertain an ideal of self-perfection as attainment of the 'true self'. It is, moreover, this ideal of self-perfection which leads them to think of freedom in terms of the 'true self' unshackling itself from the 'false self'. On this account, freedom specifies a certain kind of internal self-relation. The self stands in a potential relation of truth to itself, and the task is to actualize this potential self-relation.

One problem with Berlin's account concerns his tendency to amalgamate different philosophical positions into a single representative position. A consequence of so doing is confusion, possibly even incoherence. It is difficult, for example, to understand Berlin's presentation of the higher / lower self distinction as a metaphysical distinction in the face of his simultaneous insistence upon an overcoming of the lower self by the higher self. Its supposed metaphysical status implies the permanence of the distinction between lower and higher self. Talk of 'overcoming' this dualistic split within the nature of the human person may then be misplaced. In amalgamating conflicting aspects from the works of different philosophers whom he associates with the positive tradition, Berlin risks ending up with a phantom concept of positive freedom – one that no philosopher in the tradition actually held. Take Kant, for example, whom Berlin evidently has in mind much of the time.[25] Kant does distinguish between a 'noumenal standpoint' and a 'phenomenal standpoint' in relation to a person's conception of themselves. The distinction is metaphysical, at least on a certain understanding of that term. The first standpoint represents a person's status as a being capable of reason; the second represents the person's status as a physically embodied, needy and desirous being. For Kant, practical freedom consists in a person's capacity to exercise reasoned constraint on desire-based action. It would be a mistake, however, to read Kant as saying that in exercising such reasoned constraint a person's 'higher self' overcomes or supersedes that person's 'lower self'. For Kant, a person's rational capacities on the one hand and their physical needs and wants on the other hand are permanent features of personhood. A person's exercise of rational constraint over their desires does not result in a move from a lower to a higher *state* of personhood.

The notion of 'becoming' *is* at work in the position of Hegel – another thinker whom Berlin invokes in connection with the concept of positive freedom. In Hegel's philosophy, persons are in a continuous state of becoming. But it would be mistaken to attribute to Hegel a dualistic metaphysics of the self. For what motivates Hegel's philosophy is, in part, his rejection of Kant's noumenal / phenomenal distinction, and his attempt, in consequence, to conceive of the person as a unitary, if complex, whole. On Hegel's account, persons are in a historically determinable state of becoming towards fullest possible rational self-knowledge. In this historically determinable progress towards a higher state of consciousness, persons can perhaps be said to be superseding their previous, less highly developed states of being. But this process involves no metaphysical struggle for supremacy between a higher and a lower self of the kind that Berlin has in mind. To the contrary, Hegel's emphasis on the *historicity* of human becoming towards self-knowledge is precisely designed to keep a tight connection between humans' physical embodiment and the progressive development of their rational capacities.[26]

In Kant, we get a metaphysical distinction between the noumenal and the phenomenal aspects of the human person, but no attendant ideal of self-overcoming. In Hegel, we get an ideal of rational self-knowledge, but no accompanying metaphysical distinction between phenomenal and noumenal 'selves'. Perhaps Rousseau can deliver what Berlin is looking for. Certainly, Rousseau serves as Berlin's *bête noir*, for it is Rousseau who contends that men can be politically 'forced to be free'.[27] Again, however, Rousseau's position is more complex than Berlin is prepared to acknowledge. Rousseau offers not so much a metaphysics as a social genealogy of human (un)freedom. According to Rousseau, 'man is born free, yet everywhere he finds himself in chains'.[28] Man finds himself in chains, Rousseau claims, because distracted by superficially more attractive pursuits – such as the pursuit of desire satisfaction – man has traded away his freedom to others who now dominate his will. Man mistakes desire satisfaction – getting what he thinks he wants to have – for freedom. Yet true freedom is self-government understood as the will's non-domination by other (alien) forces or persons. In Rousseau, the notions of freedom as self-determination and of freedom as non-domination by others tend to coincide. In consequence, he tends to conceive of individual self-determination in political terms. There is a degree of overlap here with the 'liberty of the ancients'. However, for Rousseau the end of participation in government is the achievement of individual emancipation, though this achievement is possible only through social engagement with others.

In Rousseau, then, one does get a genealogically argued distinction, not between a higher and a lower self, but between a socially misguided and a politically guided self. This guidance takes the form of self-realization through shared political participation. In this connection Rousseau's notorious if much misinterpreted reference to 'forcing to be free' has done much to discredit the notion of positive freedom. It is worth mentioning Rousseau's political voluntarism, which Berlin tends quite carelessly to equate with the – contrasting – notion of a priori principles of reason (Kant) and that of rational self-knowledge (Hegel). One who is a voluntarist about reason will precisely not subscribe to either the Kantian or the Hegelian conceptions of unconditionally valid principles of reason or to rationally constrained self-knowledge. According to Rousseau's voluntarism, what is good and right for any particular republican society is decided by the general will of that society, and not by appeal to some abstract, supposedly universally valid conception of reason or truth. Yet in equating a revolutionary's voluntaristic battle-cry on behalf of his particular conception of political truth with the Kantian notion of a priority of reason and the Hegelian notion of objective self-knowledge, Berlin runs together divergent metaphysics of the self and related conceptions of rationality and reason that in fact distinguish particular thinkers within the positive tradition from one another.[29]

The voluntaristic conception of truth which one finds in Rousseau but in neither Kant nor Hegel, the metaphysical distinction between two aspects of the self which one finds in Kant but not in Hegel or Rousseau, and the ideal of self-overcoming which one finds in Hegel and Rousseau but not in Kant, all conspire, according to Berlin, to make possible the political abuse of the concept of positive freedom. Such abuse happens when 'the gap between the two selves becomes ever larger'. Once this 'gap' has widened,

> the 'real self' comes to be conceived as something wider than the individual, as a social 'whole' of which the individual is an element or aspect: a tribe, a race, a Church, a state. This entity is then defined as being the 'true' self which, by imposing its collective or 'organic' single will upon its recalcitrant 'members', achieves its own and therefore their, 'higher' freedom.[30]

The positive tradition's presumed commitment to metaphysical dualism thus enables ruthless political entrepreneurs to prise apart that distinction, and to insert, in the space originally reserved for the 'higher self', their politically preferred ideal of truth and human perfection. Doing so will enable them to coerce individuals under their political control into embracing the stipulated ideal and its political attainment as signifying the achievement of 'true' freedom.

What should one make of this thesis? Given that none of the individual advocates of positive freedom held the composite view that Berlin describes, one may well be tempted to set it aside as ideologically motivated. Nonetheless, despite its historical unreliability, Berlin's thesis of political abuse is revealing with regard to his *philosophical* resistance to the positive tradition. Berlin's deepest objection to positive freedom has little to do with metaphysical dualisms or with the notion of personal becoming: these arguments are not developed with a sufficient degree of rigour to hold much sway. Berlin's philosophical objection to the positive tradition has to do with the general connection that tradition posits between freedom and reason. Thus, what Berlin objects to in Kant's account is the idea of freedom as reasoned constraint on desire-based action. In exercising such reasoned constraint over my desires, 'I identify myself with the controller [my "noumenal self"] and escape the slavery of the controlled [my "phenomenal self"]. I am free because, and in so far as, I am autonomous. I obey laws [of reason] but I have imposed them on, or found them in, my uncoerced self.'[31] In Hegel's account, Berlin rejects the link between freedom and rational knowledge. 'I can do what I will with my own. I am a rational being; whatever I can demonstrate to myself as being necessary, as incapable of being otherwise . . . I cannot, being rational, wish to sweep out of my way. This is the positive doctrine of liberation by reason.'[32] In Rousseau, he takes exception to the latter's political articulation of freedom as self-realization in the 'rational state'. 'I wish to be free to live as my rational will (my "real self") commands, but so must others be. A rational (or free) state would be a state governed by such laws as all men would freely accept, that is to say, such laws as they would themselves have enacted had they been asked what, as rational beings, they demanded.'[33]

Whether he is invoking Kant's 'laws of reason', Hegel's 'rational self-knowledge', or Rousseau's 'rational state', the target each time is the association, differently made by each of these thinkers, between freedom and reason. What are Berlin's reasons for reacting so strongly against this connection, which he rightly detects as running through the tradition of positive freedom?

III. Reason, Desire, and the Problem of the Contented Slave

I suggested just now that when the politically motivated accusations are set aside, Berlin's abiding resistance to the concept of positive freedom turns on the strong connection he detects within that tradition between freedom and reason. In concluding the earlier discussion of negative freedom, I also suggested that Berlin's conception of unfreedom in terms of coercion supplies the key to his objection to the concept of positive freedom. In drawing these two suggestions together, I now want to argue that what Berlin finds objectionable in the concept of positive freedom is what he perceives as the coercive control exercised by reason upon a person's will. The reason why he perceives the control of reason as coercive has something to do with his radically indeterminist metaphysics of free will. Both Berlin's resistance to the connection between freedom and reason and his own metaphysical commitments come to the fore in the context of his response to the problem of the contented slave.

The problem of the contented slave is one to which a number of Berlin's critics drew his attention soon after the publication of 'Two Concepts'.[34] Berlin's response to it can be found in his 'Introduction' to the subsequent edited volume of his essays on liberty, which also includes 'Two Concepts'.[35] The problem of the contented slave raises the question of whether a person who does what they desire to do can be said to be free. As we saw, for Berlin negative freedom consists in other persons' non-interference with what a person intends or wills to do. However, Berlin does not usually talk about freedom in this way. He usually speaks in more colloquial terms of a person's doing what they want or desire to do. This implies that, in 'Two Concepts', Berlin regards 'wanting' or 'desiring' as semantically interchangeable with 'willing': doing what one wants to do is assumed by Berlin to mean more or less the same as doing as one wills to do. It is partly because of his tendency to equate 'wanting' and 'desiring' with 'willing' that the problem of the contented slave constitutes a challenge for Berlin's account of negative freedom.

Here is the problem. Imagine two slaves. One is your standard, unwilling slave who would much rather not follow his master's bidding but would prefer to do as he himself sees fit. The wants of this slave are at odds with his master's will. The slave wants to do one thing, but his master wills him to do another. Although the slave does as his master tells him, he does so unwillingly, and only because he knows himself to be under the coercive control of his master's will. This slave is unfree on Berlin's understanding of that term: he can't do as he wants or wills to do. The second slave is a happy slave. This happy slave desires to do whatever his master wills him to do. The desires of the slave are in perfect accord with his master's will. Everything his master wills him to do the slave wants to do. According to critics of Berlin's account of negative freedom, Berlin would have to conclude that the second slave is free. This is because in 'Two Concepts' Berlin talks of freedom in terms of a man being left free to do as he wants to do. The happy slave is free to do what he wants to do.

Admittedly, this slave's desires are unusual ones for a slave to have. But if being free is doing what one wants to do, then in so far as the second slave does what he wants to do, he must be said to be free.

Most people's intuitive response to this imaginary scenario is to insist that the contented slave is not free. This intuitive response conflicts with the intuitive view also held by most people that to be free is to do as one wants to do. It seems that those who deny that the contented slave can be free cannot also continue to affirm that to be free is to do what one wants to do. Either the contented slave is free, or freedom is not (merely) doing what one wants to do.

The reluctance to concede that the contented slave is free is strongly felt.[36] Yet the reluctance to deny that to be free is to do what one wants to do is felt almost equally strongly. Nonetheless, there may be a way out of this impasse. Perhaps the contented slave's desires are not really *his* desires. Perhaps the slave is in the grip of some misconception as to what his desires really are. Perhaps he has become so accustomed to his situation that he has come to believe that he desires to do what his master tells him to do. But these desires are not really *his* desires, and this is why the slave is not *really* free. On this account, only 'home-grown' desires count as freely held desires.[37] To count as a freely formed or freely held desire, a person's desires must originate with them. Their having the desires they have must not depend on anyone else causing them to have those desires. The contented slave's desires arguably do not qualify as home-grown – they seem to be derivative (in some complicated way) from his master's will. This might make it possible to say both that the contented slave is not free and that, under normal circumstances, to be free is to act on one's (home-grown) desires.

The problem with this solution is that it is not only contented slaves whose desires can fail to be home-grown. There are many conceivable examples of ordinary persons whose desires fail to be home-grown. One example may be the drug addict who needs his next shot and would do anything to get it. Another is the kleptomaniac who desires to steal the bar of soap from the shop. A third may be the clinically depressed person who desires to end it all by taking an overdose. Many people will suspect that the drug addict does not (or should not) *really* desire the next shot, that the kleptomaniac does not *really* want to steal the soap, and that the clinically depressed does not *really* desire her own death. The question of what would count as authentic desire formation arises more acutely in these examples where there is no controlling external master will that might be identified as the relevant source of interference. But what, then, is that source? Once one begins to search around for a general criterion of authentic desire formation, the one that typically leaps to mind is that of rationality. Doubts about the authenticity of the drug addict's desire for the next shot tend to be articulated in terms of the claim that if the drug addict were in a position rationally to reflect on their self-harming desires they would not in fact (or would at least acknowledge that they should not) desire that next shot. If the clinically depressed were in a position to perceive her situation rationally and calmly, she would not desire her own death. And so on. However articulated in detail, reason and rational control quickly emerge as obvious criteria of authentic desire formation.

In that case Berlin confronts a problem. He shares the intuition of most people that the contented slave cannot be free. He also shares most people's further and conflicting intuition that to be free is to do what one wants to do. But he cannot opt for the suggested solution to the problem of the contented slave. If he were to distinguish between authentic and inauthentic desires, making rationality the criterion of authentic desire formation, Berlin would risk ending up uncomfortably close to the positive concept of freedom. He would require a freely held desire to be a rationally formed, or rationally constrained, or rationally endorsed desire. Yet Berlin's central objection to positive freedom is its affirmation of an intimate connection between freedom and reason, where the latter exercises some kind of constraint on a person's wants, will and actions. This may help to explain why, in response to his critics, Berlin appears to change tack entirely. Freedom, he now says, has *nothing* to do with a person's wishes or desires. It has everything to do with the availability of options:

> The sense of freedom in which I use this term entails not simply the absence of frustration (which may be obtained by killing desires), but the absence of obstacles to possible choices and

activities – the absence of obstructions on roads along which a man can decide to walk. Such freedom ultimately depends not on whether I wish to walk at all, but on how many doors are open, how open they are, and upon their relative importance in my life, even though it may be impossible, literally to measure this in any quantitative fashion.[38]

Berlin here begins by rejecting the relevance to freedom of one satisfying one's desires: freedom is not about doing what one desires to do. It is, rather, about having options. The trouble is that, given Berlin's usual tendency to use 'wanting', 'wishing', 'willing', interchangeably, the elimination of the relevance of 'wanting' (desiring) seems to amount to the simultaneous elimination of the relevance of 'willing'. Although Berlin continues to mention 'choices' and 'decisions', freedom *ultimately* depends 'not on whether I wish to walk at all' – 'wishing' being ambiguous between 'desiring' and 'willing' – but on 'how many doors are open' and on 'how open they are'. Berlin ends up with what looks like a purely descriptive conception of freedom – one that makes no reference either to persons' subjective mental attitudes (desires, wants, wishes) or to their objective mental capacities (willing, intending). Whether or not a person is free now has nothing at all to do with whether they feel or think themselves free. It has everything to do with available options: 'the extent of freedom depends on opportunities for action, not on knowledge of them'.[39]

On Berlin's revised account, then, a person may be free without being aware of their freedom. A person may have many possible options available to them such that no one would prevent them from pursuing any of them were they to choose to pursue any particular one of them. Whether or not the person *wishes* to take up any of these options is irrelevant. But more than that, whether or not the person is even *cognizant* of having these options is now also irrelevant to their freedom! As we shall see in chapter 4, this radical solution to the problem of the contented slave – the elimination of all reference both to a person's mental attitudes and to their cognitive capacities – has been taken up most recently by Hillel Steiner, who has systematically developed Berlin's descriptive move in relation to the idea of negative freedom. Yet it is not clear that Berlin's own account can sustain such a move into descriptivism. For Berlin, too much hangs upon conceiving of freedom as a property distinctive of individuals' *wills*. Were he actually to endorse his revised account, Berlin might have to stop thinking of freedom as a capacity exclusive to persons. Doing so would make thinking of unfreedom in terms of coercion problematic. Descriptivism also renders obscure Berlin's appeals to human freedom as an especially 'sacred value'; it jars with Berlin's impassioned insistence upon freedom as that 'which a man cannot give up without offending against the essence of his human nature'.[40] Berlin's intuitive commitment to the idea of freedom as a condition of the human will is too strong for him to embrace the descriptive turn implicit in his response to the problem of the contented slave. In that sense, Berlin's response to the problem of the contented slave says more about the strength of his resistance to the concept of positive freedom than it helps resolve that problem.

When confronted with the problem of the contented slave and the consequent problem of authentic desiring, Berlin could have given in and made the capacity for rationality a criterion for freely formed desires. Freely formed desires, he might have said, are desires which are rationally endorsed by the person who holds them. Making this move would have enabled him to preserve both his intuition that the contented slave is not free and his intuition that to be free is to do as one (rationally) wants to do. But opting for that solution would have meant ceding ground to at least a variant of the positive tradition – it would have meant acknowledging some sort of connection between freedom and reason. Why does Berlin resist this move so mightily?

Berlin appears genuinely to believe the constraints of reason to be an intolerable imposition upon a person's freedom of will. Curiously, whereas Berlin is untroubled about equating willing with wanting, he appears to be strongly suspicious of positing a similarly tight connection between willing and reasoning. Quite what accounts for this apparent suspicion is difficult to say. It may have to do with Berlin's starting point in relation to the concept of positive freedom. As we saw above, Berlin presents an amalgam drawn from the diverse writings of a number of philosophers in the positive tradition. This lack of interest in a philosophically more differentiated approach suggests that his real starting point may be in what he perceives to be the political misuse of the positive concept. His personal experience – his family's escape from Revolutionary Russia when he was a child – may have been intellectually decisive. Berlin might be thought of as reconstructing the philosophy of positive freedom in the light of its perceived political abuse. In that sense, Berlin's personal experience may have contributed to his philosophical hostility towards the idea of an intimate relation between freedom and reason, between reason and truth, and hence between freedom and truth.

But there is also a second possible, less psychologically loaded explanation. At bottom, it seems to me to be Berlin's radically indeterminist conception of free will that drives his commitment to a negative freedom unconstrained even by the demands of reason. Berlin is an indeterminist not only in the sense that he denies the will's determination by the laws of causality. His indeterminism is more radical, in that he denies the will's determination or even just guidance by anything at all, including reason. Freedom, for Berlin, constitutes 'the *essence* of human nature'. To be free is to have free will. To possess free will is to possess a kind of absolute spontaneity – the kind of spontaneity associated with people's 'doing their own thing' whatever its wisdom and consequences. Herein, it seems to me, lies the basis for Berlin's tendency to equate willing with wanting, and his simultaneous antipathy towards the influences of reason: to will freely is to do as one wants to do spontaneously and unhindered by extraneous influences and considerations that compromise that spontaneity, including the constraining influences of considerations of reason.

Berlin's commitment to an indeterminist metaphysics of free will is not systematically developed. Indeed, he concedes that he cannot account for it philosophically. But from the failure to account for the possibility of free will philosophically, the truth of determinism in relation to human agency does not follow. Berlin's indeterminist commitment to the idea of free will is itself a spontaneous, deep-reaching, passionate metaphysical commitment which he believes both to be of enormous political consequence and to enjoy widespread intuitive appeal among ordinary persons:

The fact that the problem of free will is at least as old as the Stoics; that it has tormented ordinary men as well as professional philosophers; that it is exceptionally difficult to formulate clearly; that medieval and modern discussions of it, while they have achieved a finer analysis of the vast clusters of concepts involved, have not in essentials brought us nearer a definitive solution; that while some men seem naturally puzzled by it, others look upon such perplexity as mere confusion, to be cleared away by some single powerful philosophical solvent.

None of all this can detract, for Berlin, from the spontaneous, powerful, enduring and widespread if non-philosophical conviction that 'men are free to choose between at least two possible courses of action – free not merely in the sense of being able to do what they choose to do (and because they choose to do it), but in the sense of not being determined to choose what they choose by causes outside their control'.[41]

Berlin is right to think that this belief in freedom as complete absence of constraint upon the will enjoys widespread, unreflective popular support – at least upon first encounter with the idea. I am less sure that such an unqualified support for freedom as pure spontaneity of the will survives many ordinary people's reflection upon it. This is not to say that Berlin embraces a crude conception of freedom, or that he embraces it unreflectingly. To the contrary, it is to suggest that while most ordinary people would likely be swayed by the idea that a more defensible conception of freedom should surely include some constraints upon it, Berlin's position is unusual in that he denies the permissibility of any such constraints. In a certain sense of that term, Berlin is extreme in his defence of negative freedom as absolute non-interference by anything at all. This makes it difficult to avoid the impression, at times, of a certain romanticism about freedom – an unshakable *resolve* to believe that more is at stake than most ordinary people would probably be willing to concede to be the case: losses of freedom may not be quite so tragic a blow to humanity as Berlin seems at times determined to believe. Oddly, in these romanticist moments, Berlin can give the impression of being temperamentally closer to some writers in the positive tradition than the usually cooler, less metaphysically charged views of freedom held by principal proponents of the negative tradition – Hobbes, Locke, Hume. At least with regard to the passion with which he defends his freedom commitment – if not with regard to the content of his freedom beliefs – Berlin seems at times oddly close to Rousseau. This observation is not intended as a slur on Berlin's position – Rousseau is unfairly painted as the *bête noir* of the liberal tradition: most prominently so by Berlin himself. Nor is it intended to imply that Berlin was more sympathetic to the positive tradition than he gives his readers to believe. It is to suggest that, at least from a historical philosophical perspective, Berlin's endorsement of the negative tradition is unusual in the degree of its philosophical passion for the idea. Berlin clearly believed that the negative freedom tradition needed to be defended against its positive usurpers – or at least against those political opportunists who used the positive tradition for their own purposes. In part, this suggests that he took the positive freedom tradition seriously – that he understood its attractions and the negative tradition's correspondingly weaker points. Ultimately, the strength of feeling with which Berlin repudiates the positive tradition in some of its central aspects is difficult to understand. This is nowhere more so the case than with respect to Berlin's wholesale refusal to entertain or explore the possibility of a more or less close conceptual link between freedom and reason. His refusal to do so even in the face of the formidable challenge posed to his position by the problem of the contented slave arguably has left its impact on subsequent theorizing about freedom, not only in the negative, but also in the positive tradition. We shall see this particularly clearly in the work of Gerald MacCallum, whose retrieval to respectability of aspects of the positive tradition largely avoids the freedom / reason connection, giving contemporary defences of positive liberal freedom a markedly different point of orientation.

2

Gerald MacCallum: Freedom as a Triadic Concept

I. Introduction

Of the many critical responses to Berlin's 'Two Concepts of Liberty', Gerald MacCallum's 1967 essay 'Negative and Positive Freedom' has been among the most influential. Philosophically, the power of MacCallum's response lies in his rejection of Berlin's apparent assumption that one can coherently speak of there being more than one *concept* of freedom. Against Berlin's juxtaposition of the negative and positive concepts of freedom, MacCallum asserts that there is only one such concept – albeit one that contains negative and positive components alike. Politically, the success of the article lies in MacCallum's partial restoration to respectability of positive freedom, though this restoration comes at a cost. In contrast to Berlin's delimitation of positive freedom in terms of a metaphysically demanding notion of self-mastery, MacCallum's account transforms the meaning and significance of positive freedom by associating its bestowal upon persons with governmental provision to them of socio-economic benefits.

Both the article's philosophical method and its substantive political concerns reflect the date of its publication. Just as Berlin's at times rather shrill denunciation of positive freedom must be understood in the context of the Cold War in which he unambiguously took sides, so MacCallum's approach to the question of freedom implicitly affirms the superiority of conceptual analysis over alternative philosophical methods. Moreover, MacCallum assumes substantive disputes about freedom to focus on the ways in which social policies should or should not provide correctives to free market economics. MacCallum's essay was written in the context of a more generally held philosophical conviction that conceptual analysis provides the key to the resolution of all philosophical problems worth resolving *and* in a political climate in which the reality of some version of the welfare state was generally taken for granted. In what follows I want first to offer a fairly detailed summary and discussion of MacCallum's analysis of freedom as a 'triadic concept'. I shall then turn to examine his subtle transformation of the meaning and content of positive freedom.

II. MacCallum's Method of Conceptual Analysis

Although MacCallum's essay 'Negative and Positive Freedom' clearly has Berlin's 'Two Concepts of Liberty' as its target, MacCallum barely mentions Berlin. This is itself instructive. The immediate animus behind MacCallum's essay appears to lie in his reaction to what he detects as the ideological undertone of 'Two Concepts', i.e. Berlin's implicit denunciation of Soviet Russia and his seemingly unequivocal endorsement of the 'capitalist West'.[1] MacCallum finds such side-taking unhelpful in the context of a philosophical inquiry into freedom. Yet, instead of confronting Berlin directly, MacCallum speaks of the 'philosophical confusions' which the negative / positive distinction invites with regard to the general concept of freedom. In other words, despite finding himself in deep moral and political disagreement with Berlin, MacCallum chooses to take issue with the Berlinian position at the philosophical level.

MacCallum takes the philosophical high ground against Berlin because he believes he can: he thinks it possible to give a value-neutral philosophical analysis of the concept of freedom – an analysis that abstracts from substantive moral and political freedom disagreements and simply lays bare the necessary and sufficient constitutive components of the 'pure' concept. MacCallum is committed to the philosophical method of conceptual analysis. As a general philosophical method, conceptual analysis developed out of logical positivism on the one hand and ordinary language philosophy on the other.[2] Logical positivists were committed to giving a clear and complete description of (the structure of) the world as they found it: they combined a radical rejection of traditional metaphysics with equally radical empiricist epistemological commitments and rigorous adherance to the strictures of propositional logic. Ordinary language philosophers were more modest in their ambitions, believing an eschewal of traditional metaphysics *and* an eschewal of philosophical theorizing to be the primary constraints upon useful philosophical argument.[3] Traditionally lofty philosophical preoccupations were to be exchanged for the self-consciously modest if subtle task of careful analysis and explication of everyday concepts which, though they had wide currency in ordinary language use, were often employed improperly, giving rise to semantic distortions and confusions.

Though neither a logical positivist nor an ordinary language philosopher, MacCallum's commitment to the method of conceptual analysis betrays a similar disinterest in the metaphysics of freedom, together with his already mentioned belief in the possibility of a clear separation between substantive and conceptual philosophical inquiry. More specifically, MacCallum argues that Berlin's distinction between two *concepts* of freedom is indicative of philosophical confusions that result from the ideologically charged backdrop of 'Two Concepts'. A more dispassionate, formal analysis will reveal there to be not two concepts, but only one, the formal structure of which can be given a clear and complete representation. In consequence, the structure of the concept of freedom will be unambiguous even whilst disputes may rage over substantive moral and political freedom matters.[4]

Importantly, not everyone believes such rigorous analysis of the concept of freedom to be possible. Berlin, for one, does not. As we saw in the last chapter, Berlin thinks it possible to identify at least two distinct concepts of freedom. On reflection, this *is* an odd claim. Consider the concept 'chair'. There are many different kinds of chair: armchairs, kitchen chairs, desk chairs, deck chairs, etc. They differ in material substance and specific function from one another. Nonetheless, instances of different types of chairs are subsumable under the general concept of a chair. This is because an armchair shares certain structural features with a kitchen chair, and it is their common possession of these features that warrants subsumption of both under the same general concept. Imagine someone coming along and saying that while possession of a seating surface, a back, a certain number of legs, may constitute individually necessary and jointly sufficient features of one kind of 'chairhood', an alternative concept of chair is also specifiable, which picks out different necessary and jointly sufficient features. One would then be left with two concepts of chair each of which specifies different necessary and sufficient conditions of 'chairhood'. Determinate judgements would no longer be possible concerning a given object's falling under the one general concept of chair.

Perhaps Berlin's talk of two concepts of freedom does encourage confusion of the kind described. On the other hand, Berlin may not be claiming that the negative and positive traditions offer *distinct concepts* of freedom – he might be claiming only that the two traditions offer *conflicting interpretations* of the same concept. Each of the two traditions may be thought of as laying claim to the same conceptual territory – each claiming to be offering the *correct* interpretation of the *one* concept of freedom. On this alternative reading, Berlin could agree with MacCallum that there is only one concept of freedom, while disagreeing that this one concept is capable of complete analysis and clarification. Berlin could then be read as committed to the contrasting philosophical view of freedom as an 'essentially contested concept'. According to proponents of this view, a normative concept, such as the concept of freedom, cannot be treated in the same way as an empirical concept, such as the concept of a chair. Normative concepts are intrinsically less determinate than empirical concepts, in that they refer to non-empirical properties, qualities, or capacities. Their conceptual indeterminability makes them subject to perennial disputes and disagreements concerning their meaning and significance.

To my knowledge, Berlin does not himself employ the notion of an essentially contested concept, though it is a notion that has plausibly been associated with his position. By contrast, there is little room for the notion of an essentially contested concept in MacCallum's method of approach.

MacCallum is committed to the view according to which clarity is to be had in principle about any term that may legitimately claim the status of a concept. Given this, MacCallum is likely to reject as mere special pleading any talk about the less determinate structure of normative concepts compared to empirical concepts. Talk about the essential contestability of normative concepts will seem to him indicative of a lack of sufficient effort in philosophical rigour. Hence, those aspects about freedom talk which resist sustained effort towards conceptual clarification will be ruled out as irrelevant to the inquiry. MacCallum's analysis of the concept of freedom is correspondingly restrictive. In effect, MacCallum tends to treat the concept 'freedom' as though it were no different in kind from the concept 'chair'. He tends to admit as belonging to the concept of freedom only those of its structural features that can be *depicted* as such.

MacCallum's background debts to ordinary language philosophy are evident in his contention that conceptual confusion 'results from a failure to understand fully the conditions under which use of the concept of freedom is intelligible'.[5] The claim is that everyday use of the concept of freedom provides good indication of the conditions under which its use is intelligible. This does not mean that everyday use is synonymous with philosophical understanding. Everyday use can itself be imprecise or confused, and part of the task of philosophical clarification is to clear away these confusions, thereby rendering everyday use more precise. Everyday use nonetheless provides the bedrock – it provides the basic material which philosophical analysis gets to work on. Tellingly, MacCallum has quite specific such uses in mind. He does not appear to think that everyday uses of the concept of freedom invoke notions of free will, for example. Instead, he takes everyday uses of the concept of freedom to be descriptive uses – uses which describe persons as free from certain hindrances or obstructions to do certain things. The task of philosophy is to glean from such everyday uses the underlying general structure of the concept of freedom.

By way of summarizing this preliminary section on MacCallum's philosophical method, we may say that unlike some other philosophers, including, arguably, Berlin, MacCallum believes the concept of freedom to be susceptible to complete philosophical specification. Not only is there only one concept of freedom, but it is also not an essentially contested concept. To the contrary, disagreements about the concept of freedom are due to philosophical confusions which are occasioned by extraneous influences, such as partisan political commitments. Complete conceptual clarification will dissolve these confusions at the level of philosophical debate. MacCallum's commitment to complete conceptual analysability means that some of the philosophically more obscure features or components that are frequently invoked in connection with the idea of freedom – such as ideas of free will or self-mastery – are liable to be dismissed as obscure associations which must be expelled from a rigorous analysis of the concept. The upshot of these methodological commitments is that MacCallum works with a highly restricted, essentially descriptive, concept of freedom.

III. Freedom as a Triadic Concept

III. 1. The triadic relation

What does it mean to say of a person that they are free in this or that particular instance? According to MacCallum, 'whenever the freedom of some agent or agents is in question, it is always freedom from some constraint or restriction on, interference with, or barrier to doing, not doing, becoming or not becoming something. Such freedom is thus always *of* something (an agent or agents), *from* something, *to* do, not do, become or not become something; it is a triadic relation.'[6] More formally,

X is (is not) free from Y to do (not do, become, not become) Z.

MacCallum goes on to say that X ranges over agents, Y over preventing conditions, and Z over actions, conditions of character, or circumstances. Whenever we invoke the concept of freedom to describe a given social situation involving one or more agents, it is this triadic set of relations which we have in mind. Freedom statements that do not fit this triadic structure are to be rejected as unintelligible uses of the concept of freedom. In this section I shall comment on those structural aspects of MacCallum's formula which contrast most evidently with Berlin's views on freedom. These include (i) disagreement concerning the meaning of *positive freedom*; (ii) disagreement concerning the *triadic* structure of freedom; and (iii) disagreement concerning the view of freedom as *relational*. In section III. 2 I shall consider the plausibility of MacCallum's claims to the general validity of his triadic freedom analysis in the light of these specific disagreements.

i. Disagreement about positive freedom   MacCallum's principal claim with regard to his formula is that it shows Berlin's distinction between negative and positive freedom to be spurious: instead of delimiting two distinct concepts, the negative / positive distinction refers to two individually necessary components of one and the same concept. The negative component is represented by the Y variable, which specifies what preventing conditions agent X is 'free *from*'. The positive component is represented by the Z variable, which specifies what agent X is 'free *to* do' (become, not do / not become). To contend that both 'freedom from' and 'freedom to' are individually necessary elements in any complete specification of the concept of freedom is to contend that any account of freedom in which either the Y or the Z variable is missing is not a complete account. However, what MacCallum designates as the positive component of the concept of freedom differs from Berlin's characterization of positive freedom. Under MacCallum's formula, the positive component is represented by that which agents are free to do or become (Z). Z represents the particular activities that agents are engaged in whenever they can be said to be free. Berlin does not characterize positive freedom in this way. Instead, he describes positive freedom as referring to an (agent-internal) state of rational self-knowledge or self-mastery. MacCallum's very different specification of positive freedom in terms of goal-directed activity fails to capture Berlin's central association of positive freedom with a particular agent-internal reflexive relation. In itself this is hardly surprising, given MacCallum's descriptivist commitments. But it does raise the question as to the general applicability of MacCallum's triadic formula. To say, in applying that formula to the tradition of positive freedom as conceived by Berlin, that 'agent X is free from irrational self-delusion (Y) to become his

true self (Z)' is to say something that sounds singularly unin-
formative – possibly even unintelligible – in descriptive terms.
Yet it is not obvious that this result shows Berlin's account to
be incoherent: the fault may lie in MacCallum's overly restrictive approach.

ii. Disagreement about the triadic structure of freedom   Part
of what is often regarded as the novelty of MacCallum's analysis is his portrayal of freedom as a triadic relation. At one level,
the term 'triadic' simply draws attention to the fact that
MacCallum's formula contains three variables. However,
MacCallum also claims that the formula represents a triadic
relation: that is, that each of the three variables stands in a
determinate relation to each of the other two variables. This
means that any complete specification of the concept of freedom
must not only identify each of these three variables; it must also
correctly relate these individual components to one another.

   MacCallum's *triad* of variables is in some ways more inclusive than Berlin's approach. This is most apparent with regard
to Berlin's account of negative freedom. In relation to it,
MacCallum's approach is more inclusive, first, in that he
specifies one variable more than Berlin himself allows (i.e. Z),
and second, in that he is more generous than Berlin with
regard to what can permissibly be included under the second
variable (Y). Taking the second point first, recall Berlin's insistence that a person's freedom can only ever be interfered with
by other persons: non-person obstacles may render one unable
to do what one intends to do, but do not render one unfree to
do it. This restriction of what can legitimately count as a
preventing condition has something to do with the central
connection that Berlin identifies between coercion and unfreedom. MacCallum, by contrast, allows preventing conditions
other than persons to give rise to instances of unfreedom. Not
only rocks blocking a person's path, but, more importantly,
general social or economic structures and conditions may
render a person unfree to do the things they could have done
in the absence of such freedom-preventing conditions.[7]

   With regard to the first point concerning MacCallum's
triad – the inclusion of an additional Z variable in his freedom
formula – Berlin's view of negative freedom is sometimes said
to display a *dyadic* as opposed to a triadic structure.[8] A dyadic

account admits of only two of MacCallum's three variables: X (the agent) and Y (non-interfering other agents). Thus, on Berlin's account, X is free when Y does not interfere with X. Berlin omits mention of MacCallum's third variable Z – the things X is free to do. To MacCallum, Berlin's failure to specify the Z variable renders his freedom account fatally incomplete. This is because MacCallum believes that we cannot say that an agent is free unless we are able to specify exactly what that agent is free to *do*. To say of an agent that they are free without specifying what they are free to do is to speak unintelligibly. Freedom is a describable state of *affairs* in the (social) world, not some antecedently given metaphysical condition or state of *being*.

For Berlin, by contrast, omission of the Z variable is deliberate. Berlin regards the *capacity* for agency – possession of free will – in conjunction with others' non-interference with that capacity as sufficient conditions for freedom ascriptions. For a person to be free, they need not be engaged in any particular activity or action – indeed, Berlin might even reject the inclusion of the Z variable as a potentially dangerous over-specification of the concept of freedom. If doing specifiable things were to be deemed a necessary condition of being free, Berlin might say, it is a short step from there to specifying exactly which things one must do in order to qualify as free. Inclusion of a Z variable might invite political abuse and perversion in a way analogous to the positive tradition's vulnerability to such abuse.

iii. Disagreement about freedom as a relational concept
Even more important than mere discrepancy with regard to the *number* of variables admitted by Berlin and MacCallum respectively is the issue of freedom as a *relational* concept. Although Berlin's account of freedom between persons, or social freedom, has been said by some to be dyadic in structure – agent X is free when unprevented by agent Y – that account in fact presupposes a distinction between being free from others' interference in that specifically social sense and being free *simpliciter*. As noted in the last chapter, Berlin's preferred definition of negative freedom as non-interference obscures this. According to Berlin's preferred definition, freedom obtains when person Y abstains from unsolicited

interference with person X's will. But Berlin does not mean to imply that Y's non-interference renders X free – that absent Y's non-interference, X would not be free. Berlin means to say that Y's interference is the cause of X's unfreedom, not that Y's non-interference is the cause of X's freedom. Recall my characterization of Berlin's general conception of freedom in terms of the idea of an uncaused spontaneity of the will. On this view, the *capacity* for freedom does not specify a relation between persons, but refers to a property or capacity of the individual will. Others may interfere or abstain from interfering with a person's freedom thus understood. But others cannot *make* a person free.

Given his commitment to a strong incompatibilist conception of free will, Berlin does think of individual persons as free antecedently to their entrance into relations with other persons. Other persons are possible causes of a person's unfreedom, not necessary causes of a person's freedom. Yet such a conception of freedom as a (non-empirical) property or capacity of the will looks suspect to MacCallum, for whom the concept of freedom constitutes an empirically specifiable relation between agents (X), preventing conditions (Y), and goal-directed activities (Z). From MacCallum's perspective, the central difficulty with the metaphysics of free will is that it is not capable of descriptive representation. MacCallum's philosophical hostility to the metaphysics of free will is evident in his dismissal as unintelligible of what he refers to as the notion of freedom *simpliciter*. The idea of freedom *simpliciter* is the product of 'confusion and misunderstanding' which results from asking pseudo-philosophical questions such as 'When are men free?' or 'When are men really free?'[9] Berlin's uncaused spontaneity of the will is an instance of freedom *simpliciter*. On Berlin's account, persons are free so long as no one interferes with them *irrespective* of whether or not they engage in goal-directed activity. Such a view of freedom cannot fit into MacCallum's descriptive triadic formula.

III. 2. The scope of freedom as a triadic concept

Does MacCallum succeed in showing that there is only one, clearly specifiable, concept of freedom such that all uses of the concept which do not satisfy the conditions set out in his triadic formula must be disqualified as confused uses? I suggested just now that Berlin disagrees with virtually every aspect of MacCallum's triadic formula. He dissents from MacCallum's characterization of positive freedom as represented by specific things 'to do / become'; he rejects the notion of a triad of variables as involving a possibly illegitimate over-specification of the concept; and he denies that freedom is, at bottom, relational. Does this mean that Berlin is simply confused? In this section I want to examine the depth of philosophical disagreement between Berlin and MacCallum – a disagreement that does not seem to me to be the product of confusion on either side but indicative of the essentially contested status, philosophically, of the concept of freedom.

MacCallum grants that its triadic structure is not always clearly displayed in each particular use of the concept of freedom. Some uses are elliptical with regard to its structure – that is to say, one or the other of its three basic components may be presupposed but not clearly articulated in a given intelligible use of the concept. One example given by MacCallum is the expression 'free beer'.[10] Although this looks like an obvious example of an unintelligible use of the concept in MacCallum's terms, he interestingly 'translates' it as expressive of the requisite triadic relation. The expression 'free beer' can be translated into: 'Agents (X) are free from ordinary market constraints (Y) to consume / not consume beer (Z)'. By contrast, an example which does fail to satisfy MacCallum's conditions is the proposition 'The sky is free from clouds'.[11] This proposition is not translatable into a triadic structure, and exemplifies a strictly improper (if perfectly ordinary) use of the concept.

Given the possibility of elliptical but intelligible uses of the concept of freedom, perhaps Berlin's claims about negative freedom are simply elliptical in the way indicated. We saw that Berlin resists specification of what X is free to do – he resists inclusion of MacCallum's Z variable in his specification of negative freedom. But perhaps he invokes the Z variable elliptically. Berlin may not want to specify what exactly a person is free to do when others do not interfere with them; but he might nonetheless agree with MacCallum that to be free is to be left unhindered to do 'whatever'. Berlin might be prepared to agree with MacCallum if MacCallum were prepared to agree that 'Agent X is free from agent Y's interference to do / not do anything he wants to do (become), if anything at all.'[12]

I suspect that such 'translation' of Berlin's concept of negative freedom would itself amount to philosophical distortion. This can be illustrated with reference to the difference between free choice and free will. Following David Hume,[13] we may say that freedom of choice refers to an individual's choosing to do one of two equally available actions – choosing to do either Z1 or Z2. By contrast, freedom of the will refers to the individual's ability to refrain from such choice – to remain indifferent with regard to either choice. Hume himself rejects freedom of will, but allows freedom of choice. His reasons for rejecting freedom of will are similar to those of MacCallum. Both Hume and MacCallum are of the view that the metaphysically obscure notion of free will need not be invoked in order for us to be able to say all that is worth saying about freedom. In order to show that agent X is free to choose to do either Z1 or Z2, we need not posit the idea of free will. All we require is the presence of two or more equally available options only one of which is in fact chosen by the agent. Like Hume, MacCallum denies either the intelligibility or the necessity of positing some metaphysically obscure, antecedently given condition – the condition of the will's being (causally) free – in virtue of which such a choice is possible. Instead, freedom consists simply in individuals' observable exercise of choice between different available options. This Humean conception of free choice, which Hume himself calls 'freedom of spontaneity',[14] implies a commitment to the instrumental value of freedom. Freedom is of value to us in so far as having and making choices is of value to us. However, freedom is of no value over and above the value of making choices thus understood. This is one important reason why, on the Humean model, to invoke the idea of free will is to invoke a metaphysical idea or property that is as unnecessary as it is obscure: we can account for the making of choices and for the value of freedom without invoking such an idea.

In contrast to both Hume and MacCallum, Berlin is committed to a strong notion of freedom of will. For Berlin the moral significance of individual choices lies precisely in the fact that they are freely *willed*. This is just that notion expressed in Hume's idea of a will that is 'indifferent' with regard to a range of available choices. Such a will need not choose anything at all: it is free to choose, but also free not to choose. For Berlin, the moral significance of freedom as an *uncaused* spontaneity lies precisely in our wills' freedom either to choose or not to choose. This is why it would be a distortion to attribute to Berlin even only an elliptical reference to the Z variable. Inclusion of the Z variable implies that we are free only when choosing between different available things to do. On this account, we cannot be said to be free when we are not choosing to do anything at all. Thus, to try to attribute to Berlin such elliptical reference to a Z variable – a reference that merely leaves unspecified what precisely X is free to do – is to turn his metaphysically demanding commitment to freedom as an uncaused spontaneity of the will into the metaphysically less demanding commitment to Humean caused spontaneity of choice.

Does its non-translatability into MacCallum's formula render Berlin's account philosophically confused? I do not think so. Although one might disagree with it, Berlin's commitment to free will possesses no less *prima facie* philosophical plausibility than MacCallum's opposing commitment to (no more than) freedom of choice. To that extent, the non-translatability of Berlin's account of freedom into MacCallum's formula says more about the restricted scope of MacCallum's formula than about the intrinsic coherence of Berlin's position. Nonetheless, despite MacCallum's insistence upon conceptual unanimity, he does not rule out the possibility of perennial substantive freedom disagreements. At one level, MacCallum wants merely to insist that substantive disagreements about freedom are intelligible only against a background of agreement regarding the general concept of freedom. This is an important and sensible observation to make: for substantive disagreement about freedom to be productive, all involved have at least to agree that they are talking about freedom. But from the requirement that all have to agree that they are talking about freedom, the further requirement does not follow that all must subscribe to exactly the same conceptual delimitation of freedom.

Indeed, were one to require unanimity with regard to conceptual structure, the scope for substantive disagreement would arguably be severely reduced. There is something puzzling about the way in which MacCallum conceives of the intelligibility of substantive freedom disagreements against the background demand of complete conceptual unanimity. MacCallum wants to say that for anyone to be understood to be talking intelligibly about freedom, they must subscribe to its triadic conceptual structure as outlined by him. *Intelligible* substantive disagreement results from different thinkers offering different substantive specifications of the contents of the three variables: 'Instead of speaking of two different concepts of freedom it would be far better to insist that the same concept of freedom is operating throughout, and that the differences, rather than being about what *freedom* is, are for example about what persons are and about what can count as an obstacle to or interference with the freedom of persons so conceived.'[15]

There are two puzzles about this assurance that conceptual unanimity does not rule out the intelligibility of substantive disagreements. The first relates to MacCallum's claim that, although each participant in a substantive freedom dispute must subscribe to the triadic conceptual structure, they may each assign different content to each of the three variables. MacCallum merely requires that each inquirer have *something* to say about each of the three variables: this may seem like a modest enough demand. But the requirement to give content to each of the three variables restricts the content that one may permissibly assign to each. Take Berlin again: the content given by Berlin to variable X – free persons are possessed of uncaused spontaneity of will – renders variable Z redundant or perhaps even inadmissible. Since the structural exclusion of Z from the concept of freedom would not be permitted by MacCallum, variable X may not permissibly be filled with the kind of content that Berlin would fill it with. The conceptual requirement that each of the three variables be given *some* content thus restricts the content that each variable may be given.

The second puzzle is this: MacCallum claims that the concept of freedom is clearly and completely analysable. It turns out that its complete analysis shows freedom to contain further subsidiary concepts, such as the concept of a person. With regard to the possibility of substantive disagreement about freedom, MacCallum says that different views are possible as to 'what persons are'. Yet if the concept of freedom is completely analysable, why not also the concept of a person? Indeed, on MacCallum's account it would seem that the 'obvious and extremely important differences concerning the concept of "person"' should be regarded as the product of philosophical confusions which ought to be eliminated by means of a clear and complete analysis of the concept of a person. Having delivered a complete analysis of the concept of freedom, we should turn to an analysis of those subsidiary concepts contained in it and submit them, too, to rigorous analysis and clarification. Such successive delimitation of the precise structure of each of these subsidiary concepts should result in a correspondingly successive elimination of scope for intelligible substantive disagreement about the content of these concepts. In this way, the constraints regarding the filling in of substantive content which I described under the first puzzle should recur at the level of all subsidiary concepts, including that of a person.

In sum, it seems to me doubtful that MacCallum's analysis of the concept of freedom possesses the degree of general validity that he claims for it. It is a mistake to claim that all those who want to talk intelligibly about freedom must subscribe to the triadic formula. MacCallum's method of analysis is informed by a number of highly specific philosophical presuppositions and commitments which it is possible intelligibly to dissent from. One need not deny the force of MacCallum's claim that there can coherently be only one concept of freedom to reject his further claims regarding the complete analysability of this one concept. Arguably, MacCallum's insistence upon complete analysability renders him insufficiently cognizant of the partisan nature of his own metaphysical and methodological commitments. Such partisan commitments seem to me to be wholly unavoidable. Anyone who comes to philosophical inquiry into the idea of freedom will come to it with some set of metaphysical and methodological commitments and assumptions which, though often firmly held, will be contested by others with conflicting such assumptions and commitments. Though such conflicts are unavoidable, and though they typically do end, at some point, in deadlock, I see no reason to conclude that, unless such disagreements are eliminated, philosophical disagreement about freedom is in itself a sign of the unintelligibility of disputants' claims and counter-claims.

IV. MacCallum on Positive Freedom

IV. 1. Positive freedom as a metaphysical relation

The previous section focused on MacCallum's formal analysis of the concept of freedom as specifying a triadic relation between X, Y and Z. In this section I want to turn from the formal structure of MacCallum's triadic analysis to questions concerning its substantive implications. At the outset of this chapter I suggested that from a political perspective the significance of MacCallum's analysis lies in its partial restoration to respectability of the tradition of positive freedom. I also said that this restoration was achieved at some cost. I now want to try to make good on both these claims: partial restoration to respectability and the costs involved. Before doing so, I must briefly return to the metaphysics of positive freedom in general.

A large part of the substantive import of MacCallum's contribution to the freedom debate lies in his implicit questioning of the moral and political adequacy of non-relational accounts of freedom. I say 'adequacy' rather than 'coherence'. An account such as that of Berlin, which locates freedom essentially in a person's possession of free will is not incoherent. It is perfectly intelligible to conceive of a type of being who enters the world possessed of free will, who is in that sense free irrespective of the presence or absence of other, similarly endowed beings, and whose primary relations with such other free beings, once it does encounter them, is to consider them possible causes of his unfreedom. Such a highly individualistic view of freedom – a universe of individuated free wills – is neither inconceivable nor incoherent.[16] The question is whether it offers an adequate way in which to think about human freedom at either the metaphysical or the social level.

Recall my attribution to Berlin of a seemingly extreme resistance to intrusions into a person's free will at both the metaphysical and the social level. On Berlin's account, a person's will is free so long as no others interfere with it. At the social level, other agents will tend to be perceived as potential freedom intruders. Yet, even at the metaphysical level, Berlin seems given to regard the 'interferences' of reason with a person's will as a possible source of unfreedom. I suggested that among Berlin's principal objections to the positive tradition is his perception of the close association which that tradition posits between freedom and reason in terms of reason's 'coercive' control over persons' freedom of will. Hence, although Berlin's view of social freedom is perforce relational (it is not clear that it is possible to conceive of social freedom in any but relational terms), at the metaphysical level it is non-relational: freedom is a property or condition of X's will, not a relation, however conceived, between X and Y or their respective wills. Moreover, Berlin's non-relational metaphysics of free will shapes his relational account of social freedom. X's social relation to Y is articulated in negative terms: Y constitutes a potential source of unfreedom for X, implying that the best that Y can do in terms of respecting X's freedom is to stay away from X.

A noticeable difference between Berlin and MacCallum at the level of social freedom is that whereas Berlin thinks of it as contingently relational – free individuals happen to enter into relations with other free individuals and must perforce come to some mutually acceptable freedom arrangements between them – MacCallum appears to make social relations constitutive of what it is to be free. To be free always also is, on MacCallum's account, to be involved in social relations. I want to suggest that MacCallum's relational conception of social freedom is inspired by a metaphysics of freedom that is typically associated with the positive tradition. This may seem like an odd claim to make, given MacCallum's palpable hostility towards any metaphysics of freedom and his clear preference for a Humean, compatibilist depiction of freedom of choice. However, my claim is not that MacCallum shares the metaphysical commitments of members of the positive tradition, only that he shares some of the substantive concerns behind these metaphysical commitments. More specifically, I want to suggest that MacCallum's descriptive analysis of social freedom as a triadic relation is normatively inspired by the positive tradition's relational metaphysics of freedom.

Let us return to the connection between freedom and reason typically posited by proponents of the positive tradition. The connection is certainly discernible, albeit articulated in different ways, in Rousseau, Kant and Hegel. In so far as they do presuppose a metaphysics of *free will*, advocates of the positive tradition tend not to conceive it in Berlin's individualistic terms. They tend, instead, to regard human persons as members of a certain class – the class of rational beings. It is typically individual persons' *membership* in the class of rational beings that is said to warrant the attribution to them of a capacity for freedom. Capacity for reason is the ground of the attribution to persons of the capacity for freedom. This is most evident in Kant's account. According to Kant, individuals' capacity for practical reason warrants their thinking themselves free. Kant conceives of the capacity for reason as a shared capacity – one that can be meaningfully exercised only in communion with others.[17] The importance of Kant's grounding of human freedom in a shared capacity for reason lies in the fact that on such an account a person's relationship with others is constitutive of their self-understanding as free. This is evident in Kant's conception of autonomy, or moral freedom. On Kant's account, that person is morally free who acknowledges and acts, often against their own desires, on the reasoned moral demands imposed upon them by the (non-contingent) presence of others. Moral freedom is the will's capacity to act irrespective of the pull of desires and in accordance with principles of a morality grounded in reason. Both the idea of a reason and the idea of morality presuppose acknowledgement of coexistence and moral and social engagement with others.

If anything, the communicative aspect of human freedom is even stronger in Hegel, for whom freedom as rational self-knowledge is unattainable in the absence of recognition of others. For Hegel, there can be no freedom as self-knowledge in splendid isolation. Self-knowledge is (moral) recognition of others as different, and recognition, therefore, of others' existence as a necessary condition of self-knowledge. In Rousseau, who precedes Kant and Hegel, the matter is complicated by the absence in his writings of a clearly specifiable metaphysics of freedom. However, Rousseau's political conception of individual freedom in terms of self-development through engagement with others in a shared political project is indicative of underlying metaphysical presuppositions which indicate that, had Rousseau possessed a clearly articulated metaphysics of freedom, it would have been a relationalist one.[18]

The important point in the present context is this: someone like Berlin, who conceives of the constraints of reason as a potential source of interference with a person's freedom, will typically be committed to a non-relational metaphysics of free will and freedom. By contrast those who, like Rousseau, Kant and Hegel, draw a strong connection between individual freedom and a shared capacity for reason will usually be committed to a relational metaphysics. They will be less individualistic about the way they conceive of agents' capacity for freedom even at the metaphysical level. Moreover, the positive tradition's relational metaphysics of freedom impacts on the way in which its adherents conceive of social freedom. In contrast to an individualist metaphysics of free will such as that held by Berlin, advocates of a relational metaphysics of freedom will not typically conceive of a person's individual freedom in the social context in terms of others' non-interference with them. They will typically think of persons' freedom as including their moral and political involvement with others: they will view a person's (acknowledged) relationships with others as constitutive of that person's freedom.

IV. 2. Freedom as a social relation

Something like this view of social relations as a constitutive aspect of individual freedom can be detected in some of MacCallum's substantive remarks in behalf of his triadic analysis. At one level of MacCallum's analysis – at the merely descriptive level – it simply tells us that agent X is free when a certain state of affairs obtains – non-Y in conjunction with Z. However, MacCallum's analysis is clearly not *merely* descriptive. It contains a (subliminal) normative message which reads something like this: In cases where X is *not* free from Y to do / become Z, he should be rendered free from Y, thereby enabling him to do/become Z. In other words, the normative subtext of MacCallum's descriptively relational analysis is the claim that an agent's individual freedom is not the sole responsibility of the agent concerned but is, at least in part, a social responsibility. Where a given person fails to be free from certain preventing conditions, these preventing conditions ought to be removed by third parties, thus enabling the person in question to become free.

That MacCallum attributes to the positive tradition the view of freedom as a social responsibility rather than as a commitment to the achievement of self-mastery is evident from what he says about the content which advocates of that tradition typically give the Y variable. As I pointed out above, for MacCallum the Y variable – preventing conditions – can include other persons as well as social structures and economic conditions. And indeed, MacCallum associates this breadth in scope regarding the possible content of Y with the positive tradition. When advocates of the positive tradition claim that objects and conditions other than persons can render one unfree, 'perhaps they are saying this: if one is concerned with social, political, and economic policies, and with how these policies can remove or increase human misery, it is quite irrelevant whether difficulties in the way of the policies are or are not due to arrangements made by human beings. The only question is whether the difficulties can be removed by human arrangements and at what cost.'[19] Again, when considering the inadequacy of a merely dyadic account of (negative) social freedom, MacCallum says that 'it is important to know, for example, whether a man is free from legal restrictions to raise a family. But of course, social or economic "arrangements" may be such that he still could not raise a family if he wanted to. Thus, merely to say that he is free to raise a family, when what is meant is only that he is free from legal restrictions to raise a family, is to invite misunderstanding.'[20]

Although these are views which MacCallum attributes to proponents of the positive tradition, it is reasonable to assume that he shares these views. His remarks suggest that he thinks of individual freedom in the social context not only as descriptively relational – that is, as describing a certain set of relations between X, Y and Z – but as relational in normative terms – in terms, that is, which make the freedom of each in part the moral and political responsibility of some third party. Where social or economic circumstances are such as to bring it about that some persons fail to be free (from Y to do Z), it is someone else's responsibility to step in and to help ensure that these persons be enabled to be free. Metaphysically, a possible implication of this normative claim about freedom as a social responsibility may be that a person fails to be free when they fail to help enable others to be free. I do not think that MacCallum would want to commit himself to any such strong metaphysical claims. At the metaphysical level he is, I suggested, an advocate of a compatibilist conception of free choice. Nonetheless, MacCallum's strong normative views about the achievement of individual freedom of choice in the social context as a social responsibility indicate certain moral sympathies with aspects of the positive tradition's relational metaphysics of freedom. In particular, they indicate an implicit affinity, albeit only at the social level, with the positive tradition's rejection of highly individualistic conceptions of personhood.

IV. 3. Positive freedom restored but curtailed?

I have argued that MacCallum's analysis contains an important insight about individual freedom in the social context – what one might call its constitutively relational character. I have suggested that MacCallum borrows this insight about individual freedom in the social context from the relational metaphysics of freedom shared by different thinkers within the positive tradition. In contrast to those who, like Berlin, ground individual freedom in a metaphysics of free will, advocates of the positive tradition at least since Kant make capacity for freedom conditional upon membership in a certain class – the class of rational beings. This requirement of membership in the class of rational beings makes acknowledgement of others a constitutive aspect of individual freedom. At the metaphysical level, advocates of the positive tradition conceive of individuals' capacity for freedom in terms that include moral recognition of and engagement with others. At the metaphysical level, advocates of the positive tradition may well claim that no individual is free who fails to acknowledge the moral claims upon them of others.

This last is a strong claim to make. It is not one that MacCallum shares. Nonetheless, and despite his wary attitude towards a *metaphysics* of freedom, MacCallum shares some of the positive tradition's relational commitments. He simply transports these from the metaphysical to the normative level of social freedom. Even at the normative level MacCallum does not want to say, perhaps with Rousseau, that no one can be socially free unless all are free. But he does want to say that in cases where some individuals turn out to lack freedom of choice, they should be enabled to become free choosers. Enabling others to become free does not take the form, for MacCallum, of 'liberating them from their irrational self-delusions' – which is the position ascribed by Berlin to the positive tradition. MacCallum's descriptive analysis says nothing at all about freedom as an inner condition. It has everything to do, instead, with the removal of social and economic obstacles that prevent some individuals from adequately exercising their freedom of choice. It is in this sense that MacCallum treats individual freedom as a social responsibility.

Within contemporary liberal philosophy, MacCallum's is by now a widely accepted view of individual freedom in the social context. Less widely accepted is the possibility that these normative relational commitments may have their implicit roots in the relational metaphysics of the positive tradition. There are many possible reasons that may explain the neglect of a relational metaphysics of freedom even despite the widespread acceptance of relational commitments at the normative level. One is the historical interpolation, between contemporary liberalism and the positive tradition, of positivistic, and perhaps especially Marxian, social thought. MacCallum's emphasis on the removal of adverse socio-economic conditions as obstacles to individual freedom (of choice) betrays sympathies with Marxist thinking. While Marx was heir to the positive tradition, his materialist transformation of that tradition's metaphysics of human freedom may plausibly be said to have affected MacCallum's own descriptive recasting of its relational approach.

A second reason for the neglect of the positive tradition's relational *metaphysics* is MacCallum's quite independent Humean wariness of metaphysical concepts and categories of thinking in general. To the degree to which MacCallum regards concepts such as that of 'free will' as obscurantist and philosophically confused, there is reason to suspect that he would be similarly wary of references to 'the class of rational beings'. Philosophically, his translation of the positive metaphysics of freedom into a descriptive account of freedom as defining a triadic social relation would therefore come quite naturally to him.

More generally, it seems plausible to suggest that the legacy of MacCallum's still very influential analysis of freedom as a triadic concept lies in its conjunction of normative relational commitments at the social level with a compatibilist conception of freedom of choice at the philosophical level. On the one hand, MacCallum wants to argue, against Berlin, that the achievement of individual social freedom is (in part) a social responsibility. On the other hand, he locates the significance of individual freedom in persons' exercise of choice. There is no doubt that his emphasis upon the normatively relational character of individual freedom in the social context helped enormously in restoring the moral credentials of the positive tradition. Arguably, however, MacCallum's restoration of the relational character of freedom at the social but not at the metaphysical level also comes at some cost.

The cost is this. MacCallum combines relational normative commitments with a compatibilist metaphysics of individual choice. On his account, individuals are socially unfree when their capacity to exercise individual choice is compromised by certain socio-economic preventing conditions. In these situations, it is the responsibility of third parties to enable such individuals to exercise their capacity for choice by removing the preventing conditions in question. Interestingly, MacCallum fails to specify who precisely is responsible for removing preventing conditions. Significantly, he does not specify other individuals as bearers of that responsibility. It is reasonable to assume that third party responsibility rests, in MacCallum's view, with government. Governmental institutions are responsible for designing social and economic policies in such a way as to ensure the absence of certain socio-economic preventing conditions the presence of which would compromise at least some individuals' capacity to exercise choice.

From the perspective of the positive tradition, there is a striking absence in MacCallum's account of notions of individual moral and political responsibility. On MacCallum's reinterpretation of the positive tradition's relational commitments, individual persons are moral and political *patients* of governmental action. Individuals are made free by government from certain socio-economic preventing conditions to exercise individual choice. Individuals are cast as agents essentially in relation to their private choices. The realm of public agency, by contrast, appears to be taken over by government. This relocation of free individual agency into the realm of private choices represents a substantial departure from the positive tradition, whose advocates understand the idea of individual freedom as *including* notions of individual moral and political responsibility.[21] For advocates of the positive tradition, individual freedom is a social responsibility less in the sense that individuals ought to be rendered socially free to exercise their capacity for private choice and more in the sense of entailing individuals' recognition and acknowledgement of their moral and political responsibilities vis-à-vis one another. Thus, while MacCallum's restoration of the relational account of social freedom at the normative level of analysis has done much to restore the moral and political respectability of the positive tradition, his way of marrying these normative commitments at the social level with a compatibilist metaphysics of individual choice has at the same time tended to eclipse one of the central substantive implications of the positive tradition's relational metaphysics of freedom – its conception of free agents as morally and politically responsible agents.

V. Berlin and MacCallum: A Joint Legacy

The examination of MacCallum's analysis of freedom as a triadic concept concludes the first part of this book. It seems to me that no study of contemporary liberal conceptions of individual and social freedom can ignore the Berlin / MacCallum debate. Both authors have been enormously influential with regard to the way in which current liberal philosophers think about and approach the issue of freedom. Despite the force and sophistication of MacCallum's analysis, the negative / positive distinction has refused to go away. In some ways this may seem surprising, not least given the difficulties, also noted by

MacCallum, attending attempts to assign any individual historical thinker unambiguously to either the negative or the positive camp. On the other hand, the fact that none of them fits unambiguously into either camp need not mean that liberal thinkers then and now (must) all share the same concept of freedom. In many ways, MacCallum's failure to demonstrate that there is only one philosophically cogent interpretation of the concept of freedom should equally caution us against thinking that there are only *two* (interpretations of the same) concept(s). To the contrary, it might encourage acknowledgement of the likelihood that there may be innumerably many different liberal interpretations of the one concept of freedom. It is difficult to find two liberal thinkers, then and now, whose conceptions of freedom wholly overlap with one another – the idea of freedom appears to be polysemic, and perhaps for that reason capable of perennial philosophical exploration and debate. This is not to say that there are no broad areas of philosophical agreement – that there is nothing but a sea of irresolvable dissent and disagreement. As we shall see, in contemporary liberal debates the notion of non-interference is associated with the meaning and significance of freedom by virtually everyone who pronounces on the subject – but so, interestingly, is some reference to the idea of personal autonomy, or self-determination. Nonetheless, there remains much disagreement – at the metaphysical, methodological and substantive levels – between individual liberal thinkers regarding the overall meaning and significance of the liberal idea of freedom.

In the following chapters I shall not seek to come away with a well-delimited conception of liberal freedom on behalf of which I shall raise claims to general validity. On the whole, I am more interested in exploring the differences between various divergent conceptions of liberal freedom – negative and positive. As already indicated towards the end of the Introduction, with regard to current interpretation of negative liberal freedom I shall contrast Robert Nozick's account with that of Hillel Steiner: though both are proponents of negative or libertarian freedom, they differ markedly from one another, especially at the level of metaphysical and methodological commitments. With regard to current articulation of positive liberal freedom, I shall contrast Ronald Dworkin's in many ways quite individualistic account of freedom as responsibility for choice with Joseph Raz's much more deeply relational commitment to freedom as a social value. Whereas Dworkin's approach is more directly indebted to MacCallum's triadic analysis, Raz offers a much more concerted attempt to retrieve aspects of the positive tradition of liberal freedom – albeit from an unusual neo-Aristotelian perspective that bypasses direct engagement with those thinkers historically associated with the liberal tradition. But even here, when looking at contemporary exponents of liberal freedom, it will become evident that the negative / positive distinction offers at best an imperfect classificatory scheme. There are, for example, unexpected relational elements in as 'pure' a proponent of negative freedom as Steiner claims to be, and there is marked individualism in evidence in as egalitarian a thinker as Dworkin. There is the affirmation of self-creation in Nozick, and the rejection of self-realization in Raz. Whether despite these cross-cutting commitments and resulting difficulties of unambiguous classification the negative / positive distinction within liberal freedom nonetheless retains its importance and appeal is part of the explorative task of the ensuing chapters.

3
Robert Nozick: Freedom as a Property Right

I. Introduction

Robert Nozick's influential book *Anarchy, State, and Utopia* (hereafter *ASU*) is a modern statement and defence of libertarianism – a free-market-based approach to liberal society and state often associated with aspects of John Locke's political thought. Libertarians defend the idea of what Nozick calls the 'minimal state' – better known historically as the 'night-watchman state'. Proponents of a night-watchman state favour minimal governmental interference with individuals' activities, especially their economic activities. They generally regard legitimate government functions as restricted to upholding the rule of law internally and defending the state's sovereignty externally. Most libertarians are suspicious of state-enforced social welfare policies that involve the redistribution of resources from the better-off to the worse-off: they prefer to let the mechanism of the market determine allocation of resources. Their 'hands-off' approach to government reflects libertarians' generally sympathetic stance towards negative freedom as non-interference with a person's actions.

Nozick himself is best known for his provocative claim that 'taxation of earnings from labor is on a par with forced labor'.[1] Modern liberal governments typically finance distributive schemes through taxation – primarily by means of income taxation. Income tax is deducted from salaries and wages at source, without asking individual wage earners' consent. According to Nozick, such non-voluntary taxation amounts to partial enslavement. To 'enslave' wage-earners in this way is to treat them as mere things, not as persons. Treating persons as mere things is equivalent to violating their liberty rights – and violating persons' liberty rights is *never* morally permissible.

Given Nozick's uncompromising stance on distributive justice, it is hardly surprising that most critical attention has focused on Part II of *ASU* – that part which contains Nozick's alternative to liberal egalitarian theories of distributive justice: his 'entitlement theory of justice'.[2] Central to Nozick's entitlement theory is his uncompromising defence of private property rights. Nozick's theory is controversial, not only because he claims that individuals' property rights must never be violated but also because of what he takes to count as such violation – for example, non-voluntary taxation. Yet Nozick's defence of private property rights is also widely thought to be unfounded: many of his critics read Nozick as simply *asserting* that individuals have rights, including, especially, property rights. It is because of this apparent lack of justification that *ASU* has been characterized as a 'libertarianism without foundations' – as a philosophically unjustified defence of libertarianism.[3]

In this chapter I shall argue that Nozick thinks of individuals' rights as grounded in their status as free beings. I shall thus dissent from the majority view according to which Nozick's appeal to rights is philosophically unfounded. Since I shall argue that Nozick grounds rights in freedom, I shall also dissent from critics' further, related charge that he defines freedom in terms of rights.[4] According to many of his critics, Nozick begins with an unfounded declaration of individual rights and then goes on to define individual freedom in terms of individual rights. On this reading of Nozick, individuals are free in so far as they have rights. G. A. Cohen, for example, accuses Nozick of employing a 'rights based definition of freedom' – he also refers to this as a 'moralised definition of freedom'.[5] I shall suggest that this is a misunderstanding of Nozick's position. Far from defining individual freedom in terms of a prior conception of individual rights, Nozick thinks of rights as a corollary of individuals' assumed status as free beings. Of course, this simply raises the question as to whether Nozick's assertion regarding individuals' status as free beings is itself philosophically unfounded. Here I shall argue that individuals' status as free beings is grounded in his indeterminist metaphysics of free will, which, not unlike Berlin's indeterminism, treats freedom as expressive of an essential human capacity – one which Nozick elucidates in terms of the idea of humans' 'originative value' and the related notion of self-ownership.

Although rights are not unfounded, there nonetheless is a problem with Nozick's overall account of individual rights. Nozick offers two rather different accounts of rights. In Part I of *ASU* he introduces his original conception of rights as 'side constraints'. Distinctive about this view of rights is the fact that it addresses not the rights-holder directly but rather all other persons who unavoidably interact with the rights-holder. Rights as side constraints place limits on how *others* may permissibly treat the rights-holder. By contrast, Part II of the book defends a view of individual rights as a possession or power directly vested in individuals. While the first view implies that a person's status as a rights-holder is consequent upon others' (morally required) acknowledgement of their obligations regarding proper treatment of that person, the second view conceives of the rights-holder as enforcing their rights against others – basically by imposing obligations of restraint upon them. These two rights conceptions are often conflated, perhaps because they both constitute versions of what generally goes under the name of 'the will theory of rights'.[6] Yet, whereas according to the first view, a person's rights are grounded in others' acknowledgement of their duties towards them, the second view, holds others' duties towards a person to be grounded in that person's rights against them. On the first view duties are the ground of rights; on the second view, rights are the ground of duties.

In *ASU* there is a difficulty in understanding how exactly Nozick moves from a view of rights as side constraints to his seemingly differently motivated view of rights as a power vested in individual persons. The aim of this chapter is to chart this apparent shift in Nozick's rights conception and to relate it to his account of the metaphysical grounds and normative significance of individual freedom. I shall proceed as follows. In section II I shall set out Nozick's initial articulation of rights as side constraints and shall argue that Nozick's rights claims must be understood in terms of his (logically prior) commitment to individuals as moral ends: rights as side constraints are morally grounded in persons' status as ends. The analysis of Nozick's notion of individuals as moral ends will take us to his indeterminist metaphysics of free will and to his appeal, in that context, to persons' capacity for 'originative value'. The upshot is that neither Nozick's view of rights as side constraints nor his view of individuals as free beings is philosophically ungrounded. Section III investigates Nozick's change from rights as side constraints to rights as a power vested in rights-holders. This shift at the level of rights conception appears to be necessitated by Nozick's belief that the physical enactment of persons' free will requires their unrestricted right to private property – a right which does not directly follow from the view of rights as side constraints. Nozick's shift has the startling consequence that although he starts out with a metaphysics which acknowledges the morally equal status of each person as a free being, he ends up with a normative justification of freedom based on a conception of property rights which has highly inegalitarian implications.

II. Endhood and Side Constraints

II. 1. Rights grounded in freedom

In an article on 'Coercion' written some time before the publication of *ASU*, Nozick says that this earlier work 'is intended as a preliminary to a longer study of liberty, whose major concerns will be the reasons which justify making someone unfree to perform an action, and the reason why making someone unfree to perform an action needs justifying'.[7] Presumably, that 'longer study' turned out to be *ASU*. But on the face of it, *ASU* is not a study of liberty. On the contrary, *ASU* appears to be a defence of libertarian property rights. And these rights appear to be unfounded, at least to many readers of the preface to *ASU*. Nozick's opening proposition in *ASU* asserts that 'individuals have rights and there are things no person or group may do to them (without violating their rights)'. Why do individuals have rights? Nozick appears not to say.

Interestingly, the opening paragraph of Nozick's earlier 'Coercion' article already assumes that persons are free. His interest in asking what reasons might justify making someone *unfree* presupposes that persons are free originally. If one bears in mind Nozick's earlier question about when a person may justifiably be made unfree, one might plausibly read the opening proposition of *ASU* as providing an indirect answer to that earlier question. Nozick's assertion that individuals have rights and that there are things that no one may do to them without violating these rights can be read as asserting that there are *no* conditions (or reasons) under which a person may justifiably be rendered unfree. Persons have rights because they are free and because no one may justifiably make them unfree. Let me try to argue this interpretation of Nozick's position in more detail.

It will help to distinguish the view of rights as side constraints from more familiar natural rights-based arguments. Nozick's view of rights as side constraints is not a natural rights argument. If he fails to make this sufficiently clear, this may be a consequence of his general tendency, especially in Part II of *ASU*, to align himself with the political philosophy of John Locke. Locke *is* standardly thought of as a natural rights thinker. According to Locke, individuals have a (God-given) right to life, health, liberty and property.[8] Individuals' right to life, liberty and property entitles them to exercise powers of control over these domains – powers that it is morally incumbent upon others to acknowledge and respect, and which the rights-holder is entitled to enforce against others should they fail to honour the obligations consequent upon those rights. Two features about the natural rights view stand out compared to Nozick's account of rights as side constraints. First, on the natural rights view a person can in principle have rights irrespective of the existence of others. On Locke's account, had God created only Adam, he might have endowed him with rights regardless of the fact that Adam was the only person around. These rights would have been vested in Adam irrespective of whether or not he needed to enforce them against others. In this sense, the metaphysics of natural rights as a power or property directly vested in persons appears to be non-relational. It says that individuals possess rights not in virtue of their standing in a certain (moral) relation to others but in virtue of the kind of being they are – that is, original rights-holders. As it happens, God did not only create Adam. He created Eve, and through them the entire progeny of Adam and Eve. Yet, on the natural rights view, Adam, Eve and their progeny confront one another *as* possessors of naturally given rights, and the fact that they are possessors of such naturally given rights determines the kind of relations they may permissibly enter into with one another.

The second feature about Lockean natural rights is their substantive character. Lockean natural rights assign to rights-holders distinctive substantive domains of exclusive control: life, liberty (or liberties) and property. These domains of control define the scope of a person's rights and may not permissibly be interfered with by others without the rights-holder's explicit consent. Bearing these two features about natural rights in mind, when Nozick initially asserts, in the preface to *ASU*, that 'individuals have rights and there are things that no one may do to them without violating their rights', this sounds quite Lockean: it sounds as though Nozick thinks of persons as entering the world equipped with rights that are vested in them originally. The trouble is that this view of rights as originally vested powers of control does not fit well with Nozick's subsequent elaboration of rights as side constraints upon *others'* actions. Indeed, when he speaks of rights as side constraints, Nozick explicitly appeals not to Locke but to Kant: 'side constraints upon action reflect the underlying Kantian principle that individuals are ends and not merely means; they may not be sacrificed or used for the achieving of other ends without their consent. Individuals are inviolable.'[9]

What distinguishes what Nozick calls the Kantian approach to rights from the Lockean view? To a natural rights theorist, a person is inviolable *because* they have rights. On such a reading, Nozick's statement about the inviolability of persons appears tautological: he appears to be saying that persons are inviolable because they have rights, and this sounds like saying that persons have rights because they have rights. This may be how many of his critics read Nozick. However, Nozick is not saying that persons are inviolable because they have rights. His claim is that persons are inviolable because they are ends. Indeed, Nozick's claim is that rights as side constraints 'reflect' *others'* acknowledgement of persons as ends. On this (Kantian) view, persons do not have rights naturally. Rather, others acknowledge that persons are owed rights in virtue of their moral status as ends. Rights are grounded in others' morally required acknowledgement of persons' moral status.

I shall ask in a moment what precisely Nozick means when he invokes the 'Kantian principle that individuals are ends and not merely means'. It will become evident that Nozick is committed to a quite un-Kantian interpretation of persons as setters of ends – of possessing what he elsewhere calls 'originative value'.[10] Here I want to complete my argument for the distinctiveness of Nozick's view of rights as side constraints. Recall the view I attributed to Locke a moment ago, according to which individual persons enter the world as original rights-holders, where these rights assign powers of exclusive control over specified substantive domains – life, liberty, property. On the side constraints view, by contrast, persons enter the world as ends. Their status as ends entitles them not to be treated by others in certain ways. Given the requirement of others' acknowledgement of a person's moral status as the ground of rights, a person could not have rights absent their relation to others. If Adam were the sole existing person in the world, he might still have moral status as an end, but he would not need to be a rights-holder. Rights as side constraints are relational: a person has rights in so far as others owe them acknowledgement of their moral status.

A second difference between natural rights and rights as side constraints is that the latter need not specify substantively defined domains of exclusive control – at least not directly. Instead, rights as side constraints specify prohibitions on others' *actions*; they render it morally impermissible for others to *treat* persons in certain ways: others may not permissibly kill a person, for example, or torture or deceive them.[11]

Importantly, and despite these differences at the level of general conception, both the view of rights as powers of exclusive control over specified domains and the view of rights as constraints upon others' permissible actions are supportive of an underlying conception of freedom as non-interference. The natural rights view demands that others *not interfere* with a person's domains of exclusive control; the rights as side constraints view demands that others *abstain* from committing certain types of action against persons as ends. Neither view requires rights-holders to engage in the pursuit of self-mastery; neither asks that rights-holders be enabled by others to become free; neither demands that persons, as free beings, are under some obligation to better themselves, morally or otherwise. Both views operate from a presumption of the sovereignty of the free person, where respect for that sovereignty merely requires others' non-interference.

II. 2. Freedom as the capacity for originative value

I suggested that when Nozick writes that 'individuals have rights and there are things that no person or group may do to them (without violating their rights)', he should be read as grounding rights in persons' status as ends. But what is it for a person to be an 'end'? Although Nozick invokes the 'Kantian principle that individuals are ends and not merely means', his view of persons as ends is not particularly Kantian. According to Kant, agents should always act so as to 'treat the *humanity in themselves and in others* always at the same time as ends-in-themselves, and never merely as a means'.[12] Kant invokes a *shared* characteristic about them as the ground of individual persons' moral status. Nozick, by contrast, equates persons' status as ends with their individuality. It is persons' *individuality* which is to be regarded as morally inviolable.

In *ASU* Nozick is not very good at explaining in virtue of which features about them persons are to be regarded as ends. In a section entitled 'What are constraints based on?' he briefly lists a number of 'traditional proposals' for accounting for the principle of individuals as ends. 'In conjunction', he says, 'don't they add up to something whose significance is clear: a being able to formulate long-term plans for its life, able to consider and decide on the basis of abstract principles or considerations it formulates to itself and hence not merely the plaything of immediate stimuli, a being that limits its own behaviour in accordance with some principles or picture *it* has of what an appropriate life is for itself and others, and so on.'[13] The considerations conjoined in this summary convey a sense of individual distinctiveness that is focused on the capacity for self-regarding rational deliberation and action: a being's capacity to consider and decide for *itself*, to act on principles formulated by *itself* in accordance with *its* own view of what would count as an appropriate view for *itself*. But something, Nozick goes on to suggest, is still missing – something akin to 'self-origination': 'so let us add, as an additional feature, [a being's] ability to regulate and guide its life in accordance with some overall conception *it chooses to accept*'.[14]

Early on in *ASU* Nozick says that it matters to people not only that theirs are their *own* lives to lead, but also that they be able to *lead* their lives. People want to experience their lives 'from the inside'. They want to '*be* a certain way': 'what *we are* is important to us'.[15] *Being* a certain way, *leading* our *own* lives, choosing who *we are* to become is connected, Nozick says, 'with that elusive and difficult notion: the meaning of life'.[16] Some of the things which Nozick says in *ASU* about the importance of individuals leading their own lives are reminiscent of Berlin's impassioned defence of negative freedom as non-interference with persons' choices and actions. As we saw in chapter 1, for Berlin, being free – not being coercively interfered with by others in one's choices and actions – is part of the essence of what it is to be human: this is precisely why being made unfree constitutes such a moral affront to persons as individuals. For Nozick, a person's capacity to decide and choose what to do with their lives free from interference by others is similarly central to what it means to be an individual person. Moreover, like Berlin, Nozick thinks of choice as something that goes 'all the way down'. Neither Berlin nor Nozick understand choice in compatibilist terms as a person's being free to choose (compatibly) between available options. Both believe that freedom of choice includes the capacity to choose not to choose any among a set of available options: that it includes what Hume calls 'freedom of indifference'.

In *ASU* Nozick does not mention free will. He is nonetheless remarkably insistent about persons' leading their own lives, making something of themselves, choosing, deciding and acting – each time *decisively* so. One of Nozick's later books, *Philosophical Explanations (PE)*, contains a lengthy chapter on free will. Unlike Berlin, Nozick says there that his own interest in free will is not primarily to do with related issues of blame, responsibility and punishment. He is more interested in exploring the sense in which 'determinism seems to undercut human dignity, seems to undermine our value'.[17] In *PE* Nozick attempts to 'delineate an indeterminist view of free will' capable of capturing the notion of human dignity that he believes to be at stake.[18]

One of the principal challenges facing incompatibilist defences of free will lies in avoiding the charge of randomness. The charge of randomness is often the trump card thrown by compatibilists at incompatibilists.[19] If it is not causally determined, what distinguishes a freely willed act from a merely random act or chance event? In *PE* Nozick explores a possible response to this problem of randomness which deploys the notion of a 'reflexively self-subsuming, weight-bestowing decision'. He starts from a standard choice situation in which a number of possible options or reasons for action are available to the agent and where none of them is the antecedently preferred option. How are we to make sense, in indeterminist terms, of our presumption that the agent non-arbitrarily opts for one particular among these possible courses of action? Nozick suggests that there may be something about the act of deciding itself which ensures non-arbitrariness. His first claim in support of this thought is that in situations such as the one under consideration, 'the weights of reasons are inchoate until the decision'.[20] The decision as to which among the available options to go for is *simultaneously* a decision on the part of the agent about which of these reasons carries more weight relative to any of the other available options. In deciding in favour of option X rather than option Y, the agent simultaneously decides that X is weightier for them than Y. This account differs from compatibilist analyses of the act of choice according to which the choice is determined by the greater relative weight which the chosen option has for the chooser independently of their decision to choose it – say, because they desire it more.

Nozick concedes that, in itself, the idea of a weight-bestowing decision does not avoid the problem of randomness. Which option the agent's decision bestows weight upon may itself be a matter of chance. However, Nozick next introduces the idea of a 'self-subsuming' decision. In a self-subsuming weight-bestowing decision the mental act of bestowing weights upon options is part of the point of making the decision. It does not just so happen that in deciding to opt for X over Y the agent simultaneously weights X more than Y. In a *self-subsuming* weight-bestowing decision part of the reason for choosing X over Y is the *decision that* X is weightier than Y. Whereas a weight-bestowing decision simply bestows weights – possibly randomly – a self-subsuming weight-bestowing decision is a decision to bestow weights. Tellingly, Nozick's example for a self-subsuming weight-bestowing decision is one 'that bestows weights to reasons on the basis of a then chosen conception of oneself and one's appropriate life, a conception that includes bestowing those weights and choosing that conception (where the weights also yield choosing that self-conception)'.[21]

Nozick's third and final requirement for non-arbitrariness is reflexivity: 'The free decision is reflexive; it holds in virtue of the weights bestowed by its holding. An explanation of why the act was chosen will have to refer to its being chosen.'[22] This notion of reflexivity is difficult to understand. What does it mean to say that the explanation for an act's having been chosen must 'refer to its being chosen'? Is this not simply to claim that what explains the choice is the fact that it was chosen? Perhaps what Nozick means is that what explains an option's having been (non-randomly) chosen by the chooser is the fact that the *chooser* chose it. In other words, reflexivity refers not to the act of choice but to the chooser. What makes the choice in question non-random is the fact that it was chosen by the one making the choice: by the one who, in making that choice, *decides* upon *their* conception of life.

Understood in this way the requirement of reflexivity connects quite naturally with Nozick's subsequent remarks about 'originative value'. The idea that what validates a choice is the fact of its having been chosen by the chooser is suggestive of the notion of an 'uncaused cause' that figures historically in debates about free will. An uncaused cause represents the idea of a causal power with the capacity to initiate events without having itself been caused by any preceding event. Nozick's reflexively weight-bestowing decision has the flavour of an 'uncaused cause' – it has the flavour of an 'uncaused' decision on the part of the chooser through which something that would not otherwise occur is caused to occur. Nozick says that 'part of the non-random character of the weight [-bestowing decisions] is shown by the life built upon them';[23] he says that 'reflexive self-subsuming acts have an intrinsic depth' that appears to 'elude being caused by something else'.[24] When talking about the value of free will, he says that without it we could not 'originate any value'.[25] To be free is to be a source of values, a setter of ends: 'a being with originative value, one whose acts have originative value, can make a difference. Due to his actions, different value consequences occur in the world than otherwise would; these were not in the cards already.'[26]

Whether or not Nozick's account of free will in *PE* is ultimately non-question-begging is immaterial in the present context.[27] The relevant point is simply that it is only against the background of Nozick's metaphysical commitments that his insistence on individual 'endhood' in *ASU* becomes intelligible. It is not the case that Nozick's uncompromising defence of individual rights in *ASU* is philosophically ungrounded. Quite the contrary; the reason for Nozick's uncompromising stance on individual rights in *ASU* is contained in his metaphysics of free will which conceives of persons as setters of ends that are capable, in virtue of their freedom, to 'originate' value.

II. 3. Moralized freedom?

In the last two sections I argued against the commonly held view of Nozick as operating with an ungrounded conception of rights followed by an (equally ungrounded) 'rights-based definition of freedom'. I denied that Nozick simply asserts that individuals have rights and that he then goes on to assert that to be free is to have rights. I suggested that we should read Nozick as putting things the other way round: individuals have rights because they are ends, and they are ends because they are possessed of free will. On this reading it may be more appropriate to speak of Nozick as having a freedom-based conception of rights rather than a rights-based definition of freedom.

A second charge, closely related to the first, complains that Nozick's is a '*moralized* definition of freedom'. Indeed, as usually articulated by his most ardent critics, the charge asserts that Nozick's definition of freedom is moralized because it is rights-based, implying that the account would not be moralized were it not rights-based. Following the above rejection of the charge of 'rights-basedness', one might be tempted to respond that in so far as Nozick's account of freedom is not rights-based, it is not a moralized conception of freedom either. In fact, critics could make the second charge independently of whether or not Nozick's freedom account turns out to be rights-based. Even if it is not rights-based, Nozick's account of freedom may still be moralized in the sense of not operating with a morally neutral conception of freedom. So although the charge of 'moralism' happens usually to be made conjointly with the charge of 'rights-basedness', these two charges can be separated. The 'moralism' charge complains not that Nozick's account is rights-based, but that it is not morally neutral.

In general, the complaint against a theorist that they operate with a moralized definition of freedom presupposes the availability, in principle, of a non-moralized, or morally neutral definition of freedom. Yet, when discussing MacCallum's similar charge against Berlin in chapter 2, I suggested that it is not evident that morally neutral conceptions of freedom are available. Those who press the charge of moralism against Nozick often seem to be motivated by antipathies similar to those held by MacCallum against Berlin. They suspect Nozick's conception of freedom to reflect his ideological libertarian commitments. The charge is that Nozick articulates his supposedly rights-based definition of freedom in the way he does *because* he is intent upon a defence of libertarian non-distributive justice. This may be true, but it is irrelevant. In examining whether Nozick operates with a moralized conception of freedom, and whether, if he does, this is philosophically suspect in principle, it is important to set aside, so far as possible, the ideological struggles over the idea of freedom that are simultaneously at stake in this dispute.

In what sense can Nozick's account of freedom be said to be moralized? Critics object that 'if freedom is rights-defined, not just any interference with an agent limits his freedom: an individual's liberty is curtailed only in so far as he had the right to act as he did before the relevant restriction was imposed'.[28]

This objection, which does seem to conflate the 'moralism' and the 'rights-basedness' charge, implies a view according to which the conception of freedom as 'mere' non-interference is morally neutral. According to it, when we define a person's freedom in terms of others' non-interference with their movements / doings / actions, we are employing a morally neutral definition of freedom. But are we? Think back to Hobbes: according to him, we are free to do what we do until prevented from further doings by some external impediment. Is this a morally neutral freedom conception? Many of those who press the second charge against Nozick seem to think so. Perhaps Berlin thinks so (though I doubt it). Locke didn't: he objected, against Hobbes, that 'liberty is not license'.[29] Locke clearly found Hobbes's definition of freedom in terms of mere sheer non-interference morally wanting. But it would hardly make sense to find morally wanting a definition that purports to be morally neutral. Perhaps Locke was mistaken: but I don't think he was. Although it is tempting to think of freedom as non-interference as 'morally neutral', thinking this is also, for reasons that will become clearer in the next chapter, misleading.

Perhaps, when they press the charge of moralism, Nozick's critics actually mean that his account of freedom is counter-intuitive: that is, that he employs a conception of freedom that strains against common sense and can for that reason be suspected of having a 'moral agenda' attached to it. On Nozick's moralized account of freedom, we would have to say that a thief is not free to enter another's building because he has no right to do so. His critics object that it is more intuitive to concede that the thief is free to enter another's building even though he has no right to do so. Similarly, we would have to say, on Nozick's account, that a rightfully imprisoned criminal, who has forfeited his right not to be imprisoned, is not unfree. Yet it is surely more intuitive to say that a rightfully imprisoned criminal who has forfeited his right not to be imprisoned is unfree. Are Nozick's freedom inflections counterintuitive? It depends on whom you ask. If you ask me, I find the first of Nozick's usages perfectly intuitive: it seems to me perfectly intelligible to say that the thief is not free to enter another's building because he has no right to do so. It seems to me much less intuitive to say that the thief is free to enter the building even though he has no right to do so. With regard to the second example, I do find it counterintuitive to say that the justly imprisoned criminal is not unfree; yet, if the prison walls were suddenly to tumble down and the guards caught in the resulting rubble, I would find it intuitive to say that the justly imprisoned criminal is not free to leave, given that he has no right to do so. I would have no difficulty in countenancing that, being now able to leave, the criminal is likely to do so; but countenancing that likelihood would do nothing to upset my intuition that, although he may well be able to leave, this does not render him free to leave.[30] What does all this tell us about my ordinary language freedom intuitions? Possibly, that they are inconsistent. And what does this tell us about the appeal to such intuitions in philosophical argument? Possibly that over-reliance upon them at crucial junctures in the argument is unlikely to be terribly helpful.[31]

When his critics raise the 'counterintuitive' charge, they usually do so in order to confirm their claim that Nozick's moralized definition of freedom, according to which persons are free to do what it is within their rights to do, is a corollary of his rights-based definition of freedom, according to which being free is a function of having rights. His critics suggest that Nozick could have avoided his moralized conception of freedom if he had not committed himself to a rights-based definition of freedom.[32] I have argued that Nozick does not have a rights-based definition of freedom – he does not define freedom in terms of a prior commitment to rights, but casts rights as protective barriers around persons' freedom. Once one conceives of the freedom / rights relation in this alternative way, a moral freedom conception seems quite legitimate. Reciprocally acknowledged rights delimit the *rightful* sphere of freedom of each against everyone else's rightful sphere. In that sense, there seems to me nothing counterintuitive in Nozick's claim that a person is (morally) free to do what it is within their rights to do and is (morally) unfree to do what it is not within their rights to do: the owner's rights-protected freedom to own their house functions as a side constraint on the thief's freedom to enter it.

It is worth pointing out, however, that the moralized conception as articulated just now appears to bear some of the hallmarks of the positive tradition. Proponents of the positive concept of freedom, recall, posit an intimate connection between the capacity for reason and the capacity for freedom. For them, freedom has a *cognitive* dimension. Proponents of the positive tradition further tend to think of the capacity for reason as a *shared* capacity – one that presupposes the presence of others. In consequence, they often think of freedom as a shared, cognitively grounded capacity. Some proponents of positive freedom – most obviously, perhaps, Rousseau – think that the achievement of one's own freedom is a function of the achievement of everyone's freedom. Others, such as Kant, hold that one's own claim to freedom presupposes one's obligation to acknowledge everyone else's equal claim to freedom. Perhaps in virtue of its partial proximity to Kant, Nozick's moral conception of negative freedom shares, to a degree, the positive tradition's inclusion of a morally cognitive dimension. Nozick's account of rights as side constraints construes them as constraints which flow from persons' reciprocal cognitive acknowledgement of one another as free.

The real puzzle is that while one would expect Nozick's relational account of rights as reciprocally acknowledged side constraints to dovetail with a similarly relational metaphysics of freedom as the ground of those rights, his metaphysics of free will is *fiercely* individualistic. Compare, once more, Nozick's views to those of Berlin. Berlin is an individualist about freedom. Freedom is part of the essence of being human. To act freely is to decide and to choose for oneself, unhindered by others. Nonetheless, Berlin does not delimit the freedom of each from the freedom of everyone else by invoking a notion of rights. Moreover, although Berlin does think of violations of freedom as grave moral wrongs, he allows that such violations are sometimes unavoidable and are sometimes justified. Despite its highly individualistic articulation, Berlin acknowledges that the value of freedom may sometimes be more, sometimes less, significant, depending on persons' and societies' particular circumstances. Nozick's metaphysics of free will puts Berlin's individualism in the shade. Nozick's metaphysics of free will – his account of individuals as reflexively self-determining sources of originative value – contains no interpersonal dimension at all. In choosing and building a conception of life for themselves, individuals appear to be intensely and exclusively preoccupied with themselves. They appear to be unaware of the existence of others and of how others' existence may shape or affect their conception of their own life: Nozick's individual self-choosers appear to live the lives of monads.

The term 'monad' goes back to the philosophy of Leibniz. A monad is a self-sufficient, self-perpetuating, internally infinitely complex metaphysical entity which coexists on a plain with a multitude of other monads. Each monad is a universe unto itself. The problem for Leibniz was to conceive the possibility of a unified universe of monads in terms of *co-ordinate* existence between these self-sufficient, inward-looking entities.[33] His answer was the idea of a pre-established harmony among them, ensured by the existence of God. Nozick cannot similarly resort to such an idea of pre-established harmony among his individual free beings. To the contrary, his account of rights as side constraints is an account of a possible structure of harmonious relations among free beings, each of whom recognizes and acknowledges the freedom of all others. From the perspective of Nozick's account of rights as side constraints, one can think of a multitude of monads each of which is fitted with a little window through which it perceives and acknowledges the existence of other window-fitted monads. Mutual recognition makes the structure of rights as side constraints possible. Yet, at the level of Nozick's metaphysics of free will, there are no such windows. Nozick's metaphysics of free will operates with windowless monads. Nozick's monadic individuals are entirely absorbed in their own self-originating activities, utterly oblivious of the presence of others. It is this view of individuals as windowless monads that tends to win out over the window-fitted version in Part II of *ASU*, occasioning, in its train, the shift from the view of rights as side constraints to one of rights as powers of exclusive control.

III. Self-Owners, Property Rights, and Others

At the beginning of this chapter I said that Nozick works with two rather different underlying conceptions of rights: rights as side constraints, dominant in Part I of *ASU*, and rights as property rights, prevalent in Part II. I indicated that the otherwise unaccountable shift in his general conception of rights may be partly explicable in terms of the shift in focus from a consideration of persons as free *beings* to a consideration of them as free *agents*. It may be Nozick's view that if they are to realize their status as possessors of 'originative value' practically, individuals must have exclusive control over specified substantive domains in the physical world. As we have seen, although Nozick starts with a relational conception of rights as side constraints which grounds rights in others' duties, his metaphysics of free will nonetheless commits him to a highly individualistic notion of freedom which is articulated in terms of persons' reflexive capacity for a kind of self-creation. This highly individualistic metaphysics of reflexive self-choosing does not really fit the relational view of rights as side constraints which Nozick starts out with. It better suits Nozick's subsequent articulation of liberty rights as property rights.

III. 1. Self-ownership and property rights

Libertarianism is often associated with a secularized reading of Locke's political philosophy. And indeed, in contrast to the Kantian flavour of Part I, Part II of *ASU* is Lockean in spirit. Nozick's immediate targets in Part II are current theories of distributive justice. His starting point is his already mentioned claim that income taxation constitutes a form of slavery. The most distinctive feature of slavery is that it places persons in a condition of unfreedom. To claim that income taxation constitutes a form of slavery is to say that when governments tax persons, they are rendering them, to that extent, unfree. Once again, therefore, the starting point is freedom, not rights. However, rights – now in the form of property rights – follow close upon the heels of freedom – now conceived in terms of self-ownership. A slave's unfreedom consists in the fact that his or her body and will are under the coercive control of another: a slave is another's property. From the fact that a slave is another's property, Nozick infers that a free person is a self-owner. If to be a slave is to be owned by another, then to be free is to have property rights in oneself, including one's labour power. A government that imposes a non-voluntary income tax infringes upon persons' status as self-owners, thereby infringing upon their freedom.

Despite the considerable distance between a conception of individual freedom in terms of self-ownership and one in terms of the idea of individuals' moral status as ends, it is worth pausing to note the degree of conceptual affinity between Nozick's metaphysics of individuals as self-choosers and his normative insistence upon individuals as self-owners. One who, in choosing their own conception of life, is said to be involved in self-origination can perhaps be said to be a self-owner. Nozick's metaphysical thesis of self-origination forms a bridge, in that sense, between the Kantian notion of persons' moral status as ends and the Lockean view of individuals as self-owners.

More immediately important is Nozick's problematic move from self-ownership to ownership of external objects – a move that is crucial to his freedom-based rejection of distributive justice. In performing this move, Nozick leans heavily on a 'version of Locke's justification of individual property rights. According to Locke's first property argument, a person may permissibly acquire previously unowned external objects of their choice by investing their labour in them. By tilling, farming and fencing off a piece of previously unworked land, a person makes that piece of land their own. Locke's argument is generally thought to fail, and Nozick famously acknowledges its failure: why is sinking one's labour power in an external object not foolishly to waste one's labour power?[34] Nor is Nozick persuaded by Locke's second, value-added argument, according to which the investment of labour augments the value of a previously unworked piece of land, entitling the worker to the whole: why should one come to own both the value added and the land itself – why not just the value added?

Nozick's acknowledgement of the failure of the Lockean derivation of property rights from body rights reduces both Locke's property theory and his own to a theory of first acquisition. Rightful acquisition is simply first acquisition of previously unowned things. The fact that you laid claim to it first means that others cannot now claim it from you. One immediate problem with the theory of first acquisition is that it arbitrarily disadvantages later generations relative to 'first-comers': at some point in time all available pieces of previously unowned things will have been acquired by others.

Late-comers end up empty-handed. In response to this problem, Nozick appeals to a version of Locke's 'proviso', which requires that acquirers must leave 'enough and as good' for others to appropriate. Following Locke, Nozick settles for a market-based reformulation of this proviso: first acquirers must ensure that the general situation of late-comers is not worsened as a result of first-comers' acquisition of all available unowned objects. The thought is that the free-market system that emerges consequent to the system of private property rights creates new opportunities for late-comers which they would not have had had first-comers not acquired private property. These opportunities compensate late-comers for their inability to acquire previously unowned things.

III. 2. Windowless monads and property rights

With the (failed) derivation of private property rights from the principle of self-ownership, Nozick reverts to a natural rights conception. Individuals enter the world as self-owners – as beings who have property rights in their own person. Their self-ownership rights are said to entail, somehow or other, their rights over external objects of their choice. In practice, assertion of this right takes the form of first acquisition, the hope being that later generations will enjoy the 'side benefits' that are expected to result from general consent to the rights of first acquisition. But is the principle of self-ownership strictly necessary to Nozick's justification of private property rights? As indicated, even the most sustained (Lockean) attempts to derive property rights from the principle of self-ownership tend to fail: it is extremely difficult to supply a persuasive argument for the move from ownership of self to ownership of external objects. Starting from a Nozickian position on freedom, how else might one justify property rights? And what does the possibly redundant appeal to self-ownership add to such a possible alternative strategy of justification?

Recall Nozick's initial claims regarding the source of individual dignity – individuals' status as setters of ends, or as beings possessed of originative value. Beings who possess originative value are akin to 'uncaused causes', in that they have the capacity to bring value into the world – the capacity to create something that did not exist before and that would not exist in the absence of their existence. More generally, for Nozick, individual freedom consists in the capacity for self-choice or self-creation. Clearly, if to be free is to have the capacity for self-creation, then in order to act on that capacity within the constraints of the physical world, one will have to have at one's disposal a certain number of resources. Choosing one's own conception of life requires that one have access to resources necessary to realizing that conception of one's life. Note that on Nozick's strong conception of freedom as a capacity of the non-determined will, merely having access to the shared *use* of resources is not sufficient. One must have exclusive control over particular resources of one's choice. One must be able to dispose at will of the resources available to one – otherwise one's efforts at self-creation remain permanently beholden to others' wilful uses of the same resources.

The above is a sketch of a freedom-based property argument according to which exclusive control over external objects of one's choice is a necessary condition of the practical realization of one's self-originative capacity. Yet the argument makes no appeal to the idea of self-ownership. Now *if* Nozick's argument for property rights *is* a freedom-based argument for such rights, what does his appeal to the principle of self-ownership add to the freedom-based argument just sketched?

Is Nozick's a freedom-based property argument? I think that his appeal to the self-ownership principle reveals it as such. Nozick arrives at the self-ownership principle via his anti-slavery argument. What is wrong with slavery is that it renders a person unfree, and the mark of being a slave is that one is another's property. Conversely, to be free is not to be a slave but a self-owner. My claim is that *nothing* follows from self-ownership with regard to ownership of external objects *unless* the underlying premiss doing the real work is the idea of freedom. It is not because we own ourselves that we are entitled to property rights in external objects: why on earth should that follow? Rather, we may claim a right to external objects of our choice in so far as claiming such a right is a necessary condition of the practical realization of our freedom. Thus, whilst Nozick's self-ownership principle draws attention to the fact that his property argument is a freedom-based argument, it adds nothing, in itself, to the logic of such an argument. Does it add something else?

Arguably, what it does add or, rather, what it *precludes* is the possibility of conceiving of the freedom-based property argument in distributive terms. The self-ownership principle 'adds' an anti-distributive slant to Nozick's freedom-based property argument by allying itself with Nozick's extraordinarily individualistic explication of free will in terms of reflexive self-choosing. The self-ownership principle is reflexive: it posits a relationship of the self to itself. It is in virtue of its reflexive character that the self-ownership principle resonates so well with Nozick's underlying metaphysics of freedom as self-origination. The reflexive self-owner is the physically embodied counterpart of the metaphysical idea of the reflexive self-chooser. Both self-chooser and self-owner are depicted by Nozick as intensely self-absorbed and as utterly oblivious to the existence of others. At the metaphysical level, the self-chooser chooses *their* life for *themselves* in accordance with *their* principles. At the empirical level, the self-owner falls back upon a theory of first acquisition according to which acquisition of previously unowned objects can proceed without regard to where such acquisition leaves others, especially late-comers. First acquirers appropriate on their own and for themselves oblivious of the existence of others. Nor are late-comers perturbed by this. On Nozick's account, late-comers, too, are self-absorbed self-owners who acquire, if not property, the opportunities which dynamically emerge from the regime of unfettered property rights and the free-market system it makes possible. On Nozick's highly individualistic metaphysics of freedom, late-comers enter their world *as* late-comers. Being self-absorbed, late-comers will not look sideways and consider the world from the perspective of a first-comer. They will not ask themselves which world they might have inhabited had they not been late-comers. A self-absorbed, self-subsisting Nozickian monad will not compare their situation to that of others or to other possible situations that might have been. Late-coming monads only perceive, and are only concerned with, their world as they know it: and that is the world of a late-comer in which no piece of possible property has been left unowned; not the world of a possible first-comer, to whom 'all the world is America'.[35] This is why late-comers will not compare their property-less if opportunity-rich world to the propertied *and* opportunity-rich worlds of first-comers. Instead, they will take the existing system of property distribution as they find it and will make of themselves whatever they can within those constraints.

III. 4. Window-fitted monads and property rights

In allying a highly individualistic metaphysics of reflexive self-origination with the self-ownership principle, Nozick turns what might have been a freedom-based distributive theory of property into a non-distributive one. Of course, Nozick would contest this assessment of his property theory. Indeed, Nozick insists that his theory of first acquisition is the only possible *just* freedom-based theory of property distribution. In one sense the theory of first acquisition is distributive: after repeated applications of the principle of first acquisition, all previously unowned objects will have been acquired, and a certain distribution of property will obtain. But is the distribution in question a just one? Nozick thinks that it is because he thinks that it is the only distribution that is consistent with the non-violation of persons' freedom rights. Only on the theory of first acquisition will there be no interference, by others, with a person's legitimate acquisition of previously unowned objects. The distribution that will obtain will be one that will obtain as a result of the multiple spontaneous acts of acquisitions undertaken by multiple individual agents. No one will have interfered with anyone's individual acts of acquisition, and this will in itself ensure the justness of the distribution. It would be unjust of late-comers to complain that nothing is left for them to acquire, since the only way in which something could be left for late-comers to acquire is by redistributing to them some of the things that first-comers have already acquired. But to take from someone something that is legitimately theirs is to interfere with their freedom rights: and that is something one may never permissibly do. It in this more demanding, *re*distributive sense of distribution that Nozick's theory cannot be said to be a theory of distributive justice.

86   *Robert Nozick*

Is Nozick right? On his theory of first acquisition, can we say that no one is interfering with another's freedom rights so long as each acquires only what is not already owned by another? Do first-comers not interfere with the freedom rights of late-comers when they acquire all unowned objects without heed as to where this might leave late-comers? Why is *foreclosing* their opportunity to acquire not an act of interference with late-comers' freedom?[36] We saw that, according to Nozick, although late-comers will not be able to acquire unowned objects, they can acquire property through making use of the opportunities made available to them by the market system. Nozick believes that the existence of these market opportunities is 'as good as' the previous availability of unowned objects. But if it is not a necessary condition for late-comers' possible exercise of their freedom that they should be able to acquire unowned objects – if market-based opportunities are sufficient – why should first acquisition be a necessary condition for first-comers' possible exercise of their freedom? If the theory of first acquisition holds for first-comers, why should it not hold for late-comers? Conversely, if it does not hold for late-comers, why should it hold for first-comers?

The fact is that Nozick's theory of first acquisition leads to predictably unequal outcomes whereby some (the first-comers) arbitrarily have property *and* market-based opportunities and others (the late-comers) have no property and consequently often greatly reduced market-based opportunities. Non-libertarians standardly recoil from these inegalitarian conclusions: they find it difficult to accept that a distribution with such predictably unequal outcomes could be characterized as just. Many further conclude that Nozick's libertarian argument demonstrates the non-availability of a freedom-based theory of just distribution – at least if one understands by the latter some form of egalitarian distribution. Many tend to equate libertarianism in practice *and* in theory with disdain for egalitarian concerns.

There is, it seems to me, good historical reason for associating libertarianism with unconstrained free-market politics and consequent deep social inequalities. It is less clear whether their admittedly often obsessive preoccupation with negative individual freedom renders libertarians incapable, in principle, of acknowledging demands of social equality. Take Berlin, whose preference for negative individual freedom among other commitments places him broadly within the libertarian camp. Berlin clearly does think of redistributive policies as freedom constraining, and he is for that reason wary of them. Nonetheless, Berlin equally clearly believes such freedom-constraining redistributive policies to be morally desirable at least some of the time. Berlin simply insists that such redistributive policies should not be urged in the name of 'greater freedom', but should be urged, instead, in the name of the conflicting value of greater social equality.

On the other hand, many non-libertarians believe a concern with social equality to be an integral part of a concern with freedom:[37] while redistributive policies may indeed reduce the freedom of the better-off (Nozick's first-comers), they also increase the freedom of the worse-off (Nozick's late-comers). Libertarianism is thought to be incapable of acknowledging this. Libertarianism regards redistribution with suspicion because it tends to assume that redistributive policies always represent incursions into the freedom of some for the sake of the *equality* interests of others, not their freedom interests. As we saw in chapter 2, this is questionable. But even if libertarians perceive *redistribution* to be problematic, they should not find an equal initial *distribution* problematic. To the contrary, libertarians should surely judge morally requisite an equal initial distribution of negative freedom: if each has a right to negative freedom, then each surely has an equal right to it. If Nozick's entitlement theory of justice turns out to be highly unequal in its distribution of the means necessary to the exercise of negative freedom, this is probably a consequence of his highly individualistic conception of freedom in terms of self-creation in conjunction with the self-ownership principle and the ill-fated labour theory of property. Arguably, however, such excessive individualism need not be a feature of libertarianism. A less individualistic metaphysics of free will, one operating, minimally, with a conception of window-fitted monads, could, in conjunction with the view of rights as side constraints, have yielded an argument which acknowledged the equal right of each to access to the means necessary to the exercise of their moral status as ends, or as setters of ends. This is essentially the freedom-based property argument sketched above, which made no reference to the principle of self-ownership. Conjoined with the relational view of side constraints, it may be restated as follows: in so far as rights are conceived as a corollary of others' acknowledgement of a person's moral status as an end, property rights may be thought of as following from others' acknowledgement of the legitimacy of a person's claim to resources as a necessary condition of the practical realization of their moral status as a setter of ends. Or, putting it the other way around: anyone who lays claim, in virtue of their status as a free agent, to possession of external objects necessary to the practical realization of that status must acknowledge the equally valid claim to such possession on the part of all other beings with such status. On this argument, the freedom-based right to acquisition by any one agent would be constrained by that agent's acknowledgement of the equal freedom-based right to acquisition by all others. The fact that Nozick himself did not end up going down the road of a freedom-based justification of *equal* property rights has not prevented others from detecting elements in his position that invite such an alternative libertarian argument. Foremost among these egalitarian libertarian arguments in favour of equal property rights is that of Hillel Steiner, whose theory of equal libertarian freedom is the subject matter of the next chapter.

4

Hillel Steiner: The Equal Natural Right to Pure Negative Liberty

I. Introduction

Although libertarianism is often associated with 'right-wing' liberal politics, libertarians are not right-wing in the sense of being conservative: they do not insist upon the wisdom of received traditions; nor do they promote the ideal of the national community over more individualistic values and aspirations. Instead, libertarians are said to be right-wing in the sense of being anti-egalitarian. They are said to reject 'left-wing' redistributive policies, preferring to let the market determine the allocation of resources. Relatedly, they are also said to promote a particularly virulent form of individualism – one that regards society as a mere by-product of multiple individual interactions and exchanges.

Libertarianism provokes strong responses: people tend either to embrace or to repudiate the theory in its entirety. There is no room for middle ground – libertarian philosophers are conviction theorists as much as libertarian practitioners are said to be conviction politicians. 'Individuals have rights', says Nozick, 'and there are things one must not do to them without violating their rights.' For Nozick, there must *never* be a trade-off between individual rights and other moral values or social concerns, no matter what the consequences.[1] Libertarians combine such moral rigorism with an equally vigorous style of philosophical argumentation in which boldly

stated premisses are pushed through chains of inferential reasoning to their logically inescapable conclusions. There is
something exhilarating about this style of argumentation –
though many also find misguided the tendency to equate
moral reasoning with serial logical deduction. Still, proponents of right-wing libertarianism and their detractors agree
on at least one thing: they agree that the libertarian creed is
fundamentally anti-egalitarian.

This last is the view which Hillel Steiner dissents from.
Steiner is a left-libertarian who advocates an egalitarian form
of libertarianism. According to him, individuals have an *equal*
natural right to (negative) freedom. Although this is a familiar libertarian premiss, Steiner unusually interprets it in substantive distributive terms. To assert that individuals have an
equal natural right to freedom implies, on Steiner's reading, a
substantive libertarian requirement to distribute freedom
equally among individuals.[2] But how is such an equal distribution of freedom possible? Through the deployment of a
highly unusual conception of negative freedom. Steiner calls it
'pure negative freedom', and he associates it with Hobbes and
Bentham but also, more unusually, with Kant. He claims that
'pure negative freedom' offers a descriptive account of
freedom which, in so far as it excludes from consideration all
reference to agents' inner mental states, must be contrasted
with evaluative approaches to freedom. The principal advantage of such a non-evaluative, purely descriptive account is
the possible articulation of freedom as a quantifiable good
capable of an equal distribution.

We encountered one attempt to provide a descriptive
account of freedom in MacCallum's analysis of freedom as a
unitary, triadic concept the practical realization of any
particular instance of which requires the satisfaction of relevant, empirically specifiable enabling conditions that render
the observable enjoyment of specific freedoms equally accessible to all. However, Steiner's descriptive approach is
motivated by assumptions and concerns different from those
of MacCallum. For one thing, Steiner does not reject the
negative / positive distinction. He is a strident advocate of negative freedom who believes others' non-interference with a
person's action to be a necessary and sufficient condition
of that person's being free to do the action. Besides, Steiner's

principal philosophical concerns are normative rather than methodological. Steiner adopts a descriptive freedom approach because he is concerned to operationalize negative freedom as a quantifiable good.[3] Underlying Steiner's descriptive approach to negative freedom is his interest in designing, in critical reaction to Nozick, a theory of libertarian distributive justice which assigns to individuals equal natural property rights, issuing in what Steiner refers to as a (determinate) set of compossible rights.

Even as a left-libertarian Steiner shares with Nozick certain basic libertarian premises. He shares Nozick's commitment to the principle of self-ownership, and his view that individuals have a natural right to private property – though, unlike Nozick, Steiner does not derive the latter from the former.[4] More generally, Steiner is committed to a rights-based morality: his preference for the idea of negative freedom as non-interference is largely explicable in terms of this general commitment to the idea of rights. Yet Steiner also contends that his account of negative freedom is 'purer' than the accounts of either Berlin or Nozick, in that it eliminates from the negative conception all evaluative connotations that in his view still contaminate these earlier approaches. The principal question to be addressed in the present chapter is to what extent Steiner is able to make good on this claim. How 'pure' – in the descriptive sense – is Steiner's account? I shall suggest that while Steiner offers a highly *formalized* account of negative freedom, which does indeed differ from more substantive libertarian approaches, his is not in the end a purely *descriptive* account. To the contrary, Steiner's theory remains reliant upon a formal yet nonetheless broadly normative presumption in favour of the claim to freedom as the ground of individuals' entitlements and obligations.[5] In the next section I begin with some remarks on Hobbes and Kant as the two most important philosophical precursors to Steiner's position, and then go on to outline his account of pure negative freedom. Section III assesses the plausibility of Steiner's contention to be eschewing reference to evaluative attitudes and capacities, reaching partially negative conclusions in this regard. Section IV bolsters these conclusions by arguing that Steiner's account of property rights as a type of freedom rights cannot get off the ground without a crucial normative presumption concerning the relational character of these rights. Section V draws more general conclusions regarding the limitations of a purely descriptive approach to (negative) freedom.

II. Pure Negative Freedom Outlined

II. 1. Historical preliminaries: Hobbes versus Kant

Steiner shares with Nozick two basic Lockean premisses: the principle of self-ownership and the thesis of individuals' natural entitlement to private property. Yet, like Nozick, Steiner additionally draws on Kant, although he does so in ways that are very different from those of Nozick. Steiner's appeal to Kant is an inflection of his broader sympathies with Hobbes. To many readers this marriage of Hobbes and Kant may seem counterintuitive, given the usual association of Hobbes with a physicalist conception of freedom in contrast to Kant's normative approach. However, Kant distinguishes between what he calls 'internal freedom' and 'external freedom' – one might translate this as 'moral freedom' and 'political freedom', respectively. Kant's account of internal freedom is the one standardly associated with his name: freedom as a form of reason-governed, inner self-legislation. By contrast, his lesser-known conception of external freedom is a version of negative freedom: freedom as non-interference by others. It is this latter conception that Steiner appeals to, and this reduces the gap between the Hobbesian and Kantian accounts.

Yet, although the gap is reduced, it should not be eliminated. Recall that, for Hobbes, freedom is simply an object's being in a state of externally unimpeded motion. Water hurtling down a stream, a rock falling off a cliff, a man walking along a highway – these are all instances of objects in unimpeded motion. In chapter 1 I suggested that even for Hobbes the absence of external impediments is a necessary, not a sufficient, condition of freedom. To qualify as free, objects have to be in some state of self-induced motion. The water in the stream is propelled forward by its current, the rock is propelled downward by its weight, and the man is propelled onwards by his desires. Nonetheless, self-induced motion is conceived mechanically: none of the objects in question possesses any extra-physical control over that force within them in virtue of which they find themselves in motion. Freedom interferences are likewise thought of in strictly physicalist terms. Hobbes does not require freedom interferences to be deliberate or intentional in character. A freedom interference is simply a physical prevention: a boulder lying across the road interferes with a person's freedom to travel down the road every bit as much as a group of highwaymen do who place themselves in the person's way.

In contrast to Hobbes, Kant conceives of a person's capacity for external freedom in terms of their rational capacity for self-directed choice and action, where this rational capacity is not reducible to a physicalist explanation. Kant's distinction between the physical world of natural causality and the moral world of reason is well known.[6] Less often noted is his relational conception of the world of reason. I drew attention to this already in chapter 2 when talking about the positive tradition's tendency to conceive of reason as a shared capacity, i.e. as a capacity which we each possess and exercise in community with others. For Kant, just as the physical world is governed by laws of natural causality, so the moral world, the world of reason, is governed by the laws of reason. The nomological character of this world of reason implies its relational structure: each member of the world of reason is conceived as standing in a law-governed relation with all other members. In the present context, an important corollary of this general feature of Kant's metaphysics of morals is this: in so far as Kant conceives of external freedom as presupposing a rational capacity for choice and action, and in so far as he conceives of the capacity for rationality in law-governed, relational terms, then external freedom, too, must be a law-governed, relational capacity. Hence, being externally free is a function, for Kant, of a twofold requirement: on the one hand, an agent must possess the rational capacity for self-directed choice and action; on the other hand, other agents must recognize the agent as possessing such a capacity and must acknowledge that capacity as a constraint upon their own actions. Ultimately, for Kant, an agent's external freedom is a function of other agents' deliberate non-interference with the agent's recognized capacity for rationally self-directed choice and action.[7]

It is this requirement of others' irreducibly *deliberate* non-interference with a person's irreducibly *rational* capacity for choice and action which sets Kant's account of external freedom apart from Hobbesian physicalism, giving it its normative character. If it is nonetheless tempting to assimilate Kant's normative account to a descriptive account, this is a consequence, in part, of the highly formal character of Kant's non-descriptivism. Importantly, Kant abstracts from the particular evaluative reasons which any agent may have for refraining from interfering with another's power of choice. For example, I may deliberately refrain from interfering with another's power of choice because I fear the possibly adverse consequences of interfering. Alternatively, I may deliberately so refrain because I acknowledge that it would be wrong of me to interfere. Or again, I may so refrain because interfering would not in any case get me what I want. Each of these examples includes a reference to a possible subjective reason for non-interference on my part which is decisive for my not interfering in any given instance. Yet Kant considers none of these possible subjective reasons for self-restraint vis-à-vis another's freedom as relevant to determining the requirements, in general, of external freedom relations: the only relevant requirement is, for Kant, the capacity for deliberate non-interference in general.

Steiner's aim to develop a descriptive account of freedom as a quantifiable good capable of an equal distribution encourages him to conflate Hobbes's descriptive physicalism with what I shall refer to as Kant's normative formalism. In part, the conflation is a consequence of Steiner's views about what an evaluative freedom conception amounts to. As we shall see in more detail below, Steiner assumes that any evaluative approach to freedom will include reference to persons' subjective evaluative attitudes – that is, to their subjectively held desires, feelings and intentions. Hence Steiner might be taking Kant's explicit abstraction from subjective evaluative reasons to be indicative of his descriptivism. Steiner thus elides the distinction between his descriptive approach and Kant's normative formalism, allowing him to subsume the latter under his own approach. Yet it is precisely Steiner's assimilation of

Kant's normative formalism to his own descriptivism that eventually raises the question of how 'pure' Steiner's descriptivism is ultimately. Before turning to this question, it is necessary to sketch an overview of Steiner's theory of pure negative freedom.

II. 2. Pure negative freedom and the possession of things

Chapter 1 of Steiner's *An Essay on Rights*, entitled 'Liberty', begins with a candid acknowledgement of the semantic diversity of everyday uses of the term 'freedom' – a diversity which reflects the fact that we have multiple, often conflicting, freedom intuitions, yielding semantic divergences that we nonetheless manage to negotiate perfectly intelligibly in everyday usage of the concept. Nonetheless, and despite the manageability of everyday semantic diversity, when constructing a philosophical theory of freedom, Steiner takes consistency requirements to be of paramount importance. At the philosophical level we must 'expel' or 'silence' some of our conflicting ordinary intuitions about freedom so as to ensure the requisite degree of terminological consistency.[8] Since such expulsion is never easy, we should, 'in picking and choosing among our intuitions take some care to silence only those intuitions whose absence from our usage promises to cause us less discomfort than would be the absence of those it continues to reflect'.[9] We should retain only those intuitions which we find hardest to give up.

The intuition which Steiner himself finds hardest to give up is that 'persons are free to do what they actually do'.[10] Steiner thinks that this is a rudimentary descriptive freedom intuition that is beyond need of justification. Yet he immediately adds that '[persons are] also free to do many of the things they don't do and would never consider doing'. This qualification complicates matters considerably. The inclusion of things one could but doesn't do invokes the category of 'possible action', introducing modalities which do not figure in the initial rudimentary intuition. Crucially, Steiner thinks that his two intuitions – doing what one *actually* does, and not doing what one *could do* – come to the same thing. Having stated them, he declares that 'the rest of the chapter is devoted to looking at some of the implications of an unswerving commitment to those ideas'. The definition of pure negative freedom follows abruptly: 'a person is unfree to do an action if, and only if, his doing that action is rendered impossible by the action of another person'.[11]

As a general definition of negative freedom, Steiner's formulation should by now sound familiar. Both Berlin and Nozick conceive of negative freedom in superficially similar ways. Both predicate freedom only of persons, and both share the view that only other persons can render one unfree. However, Steiner claims that his definition of negative freedom is pure in a way in which Berlin's and Nozick's respective accounts fail to be. For both Berlin and Nozick, others' *coercive* interferences with a person's power of *will* constitute paradigmatic instances of unfreedom. A person is unfree when another gets them to do what they would not otherwise do by bringing about a change at the level of their intentions. The 'impurity' of these conceptions of (un)freedom lies in the pivotal role they assign to what Steiner perceives as a reference to persons' subjective mental states. Steiner believes that the inclusion of mentalistic references to agents' intentions renders Berlin's and Nozick's respective negative freedom accounts evaluative in the sense of the term which he rejects. Hence the reference, in Steiner's definition, to 'rendering a person's action impossible' is not to be understood 'mentalistically' – that is, in terms of someone's exerting non-physical pressure on another's power of will. Instead, it is to be thought of in strictly physical terms.

In Steiner's account, 'rendering impossible' is to be understood as referring to another's *physical prevention* of a person's actions. To be unfree to do X is to be physically prevented by another from doing X. Conversely, to be free to do X is to be physically unprevented by another from doing X. This sounds very Hobbesian, although, in contrast to Hobbes, Steiner unaccountably restricts physicalist relations of freedom and unfreedom to *persons*, excluding streaming water and falling rocks, etc. Recall the example of the highwaymen from chapter 1, who threaten the traveller with the demand, 'Your money or your life!' For Berlin and Nozick the traveller's freedom is interfered with at the point of the highwaymen's issuing their threat: the traveller's unfreedom consists in the highwaymen's exertion of coercive pressure upon the traveller's intentions. Yet Steiner denies that threats render a person unfree: to threaten someone is not to prevent them *physically*. On Steiner's pure negative account, it is only at the point at which the highwaymen physically prevent the traveller from proceeding – by tying him to a tree, or by sticking a knife in his chest – that they make him unfree.[12]

Imagine, on the other hand, our traveller walking down the road and not encountering a group of highwaymen. The path is clear, the sun is shining – everything is unperturbed. On this scenario the traveller is physically unprevented by others from continuing along the road. He is free in the specific sense that his being physically unprevented by others entails his being in possession of the relevant 'action space'. To be unpreventedly free to do an action is to be in possession of all the physical components required for performing the action. With each step he takes down the road, the traveller is in physical possession of those bits of the road which his body occupies as he moves along. The traveller feels hungry. He approaches an apple tree by the side of the road, picks an apple and eats it. Because he was in physical possession of access to the apple tree, because he came to be in physical possession of the apple which he ate, he was free to eat the apple. Later the traveller sets up camp for the night. He makes himself a bed from straw in a field, lights a fire with wood from the adjacent forest, gathers mushrooms from the undergrowth for his omelette (he carried the eggs with him in his bag). Straw, wood, mushrooms: being in physical possession of all these things means that the traveller is free to do all these actions.

'Freedom', Steiner asserts, 'is the possession of things.' More formally, 'prevention is a relation between the respective actions of two persons such that the occurrence of one of them rules out the occurrence of the other'.[13] Hence 'I am unfree to do an action if control of at least one of its physical components is actually or subjunctively denied me by another person' (I shall deal with the notion of 'subjunctive possession' in section IV below).[14] Steiner thus moves from an initially undemanding Hobbesian conception of freedom as physical non-prevention to a considerably more demanding conception of freedom as the possession of things. In the case of the traveller and the highwaymen, the traveller's freedom to carry on down the road depends on his being in possession of the physical components necessary to perform the action of carrying on down the road. At the point at which the highwaymen physically prevent the traveller from proceeding, possession of the relevant 'action space' passes from traveller to highwaymen. At this descriptive level, Steiner's account of negative freedom is strictly relational: my being free to do X entails your being unfree to do X. 'Doing X' is analysed quantitatively into 'possessing all of the physical components necessary for doing X'. My being free to do X and your being correspondingly unfree to do X can therefore also be rendered as my being in possession of all the physical components necessary to the doing of X, in contrast to your lacking such possession.

Recall Steiner's libertarian premiss – the equal natural right to freedom – and the distributive demand he thinks entailed by it. In so far as we do each have an equal right to freedom, the free actions undertaken by each of us must be 'compossibly' performable with the free actions undertaken by all others of us: we must all be able to be free simultaneously. If freedom is the possession of things, then none of the free actions which I engage in must contain any of the physical components required for your engaging in your free actions. In the case of a two-person freedom relation, 'two actions, A and B, are incompossible if there is partial coincidence between the extensional description of A and (. . .) B's extensional description'.[15] To be both freely performable, actions A and B must be compossible, and to be compossible, the physical components necessary to doing A must not overlap with those necessary to doing B.

The compossibility requirement entailed by the equal freedom right allows Steiner to make the further move from freedom as the possession of things to freedom as a property right in things. The compossibility requirement is satisfied when the action space of each is secured against intrusion by others. The securement of each person's action space against intrusion by all others is achieved through the assignment to each person of a property right in their action space. 'A set of categorically compossible domains [i.e. 'action spaces'], constituted by a set of property rights, is one in which each person's rights are demarcated in such a way as to be mutually exclusive of every other person's rights. This means that no two persons can simultaneously have rights to one and the same physical thing.'[16] Since all have an equal natural right to freedom, what each is naturally entitled to is an equal share in the earth's natural resources. Each of us, upon entrance into the world, is entitled to exclusive possession of an equal share of the earth's natural resources.

Quite how Steiner envisages the practical task of equally dividing and distributing the earth's natural resources among individual members of succeeding generations need not concern us here. But contrast, briefly, Steiner's libertarian egalitarianism with Nozick's inegalitarian position on the one hand and with non-libertarian egalitarianism on the other. Recall Nozick's more orthodox Lockean account of an (obscure) connection between self-ownership and ownership of external objects. It is essentially this perceived connection between these two kinds of ownership which results in a highly inegalitarian distribution of property rights between early birds and late-comers: early birds appropriate by investing their labour with the unavoidable consequence that late-comers end up empty-handed. Conceptually, Steiner's solution is much more elegant: instead of attempting to derive rights in external objects from the self-ownership principle, his physicalist account of pure negative freedom as amounting to a property right in things underwrites the claim to an equal distribution of the earth's natural resources as a direct corollary of the equal natural right to freedom of each. We have here a version of a freedom-based property argument that makes no reference to the contentious posited connection between self-ownership and ownership of external things. Nonetheless, Steiner does not abandon the self-ownership principle. When a person mixes their labour with the stock of natural resources to which they are originally entitled, the resulting value added is the labourer's exclusive possession and cannot justly be made subject to redistribution. Unlike more radical *redistributive* egalitarian positions, Steiner's equality of starting points does not result in an equality of outcomes, nor is it intended to. Although each person starts off with an equal amount of natural resources, what they each end up doing with their resources – whether they augment or squander them – is up to them. There can be, on Steiner's account, considerable degrees of justified social economic inequality against a background of the morally required natural (economic) equality.

III. Pure Negative Freedom: Descriptive or Evaluative?

Libertarianism, I said, provokes strong responses. Nozick's and Steiner's respective theories are cases in point – though for different reasons. While the publication of *ASU politically* scandalized many of Nozick's more egalitarian-minded philosophical peers, the reaction against Steiner's position is more one of *conceptual* incredulity: could anyone seriously entertain the pure negative conception of freedom? Most people probably still answer this question in the negative; nonetheless, a growing minority of liberal philosophers find great promise in Steiner's descriptive approach to the measurability of freedom as a distributive good.[17] In this section and the next I shall query the extent of Steiner's descriptivism. I shall suggest that what account for the originality and elegance of Steiner's account are at least in part certain presuppositions regarding persons' formal normative capacities. I shall divide my argument into two steps, arguing, in this section, that Steiner's contrast between descriptive and evaluative approaches to freedom is too narrow and, in section IV, that his move from freedom as physical non-prevention to freedom as a property right represents a move from a Hobbesian descriptivism to a Kantian normative formalism about freedom.

First, then, what explains Steiner's hostility to what he calls evaluative approaches to freedom? One factor is obvious: evaluative judgements are qualitative rather than quantitative in kind. Given his distributive concerns, Steiner requires a quantitative approach. But if this is what Steiner requires, what makes him think that he can have it? The short answer is that Steiner thinks it possible to distinguish the *fact* of freedom from its *value*. More specifically, he believes that one can distinguish analytically between 'being free' and 'feeling free', where being free refers to the descriptive dimension of freedom, whereas feeling free is its evaluative dimension.

Indeed, Steiner believes that the problem of the contented slave demonstrates the *necessity* of distinguishing between being free and feeling free. Recall the problem of the contented slave, who is free to do whatever he desires to do. This problem arose in connection with Berlin's initial characterization of negative freedom in terms of a person's being free to do what they want to do. On Berlin's initial definition of negative freedom we are compelled to admit that the contented slave is free. Recall further Berlin's solution to the problem. Given his hostility towards the positive connection between freedom and reason, Berlin was unable to endorse the view according to which to be free is to act on one's rational desires, or on one's rationally endorsed desires. Instead, Berlin made the extent of a person's freedom a function of how many options are available to them. This essentially descriptive move seemed at odds with Berlin's earlier emphasis upon freedom as a property of the individual will, incompatibly conceived.

The notion that the extent of a person's freedom is a function of how many 'doors' are open to them is not, on the face of it, a strange move to make for one who is in any case committed to descriptivism about freedom. Unlike Berlin, Steiner is not pushed into making the descriptive move as a result of the problem of the contented slave. To the contrary, he takes that problem to confirm the need to distinguish between description and evaluation – between being free and feeling free. The problem of the contented slave shows us, Steiner thinks, that however free the slave may *feel*, he is unfree in matter of *fact*: the slave is simply mistaken in his evaluative freedom judgement about his actual freedom situation. Steiner quietly introduces a series of pairwise distinctions. There is, first, the distinction between being free and feeling free. This is equated with the distinction between description and evaluation. The latter is treated as equivalent, in turn, to the distinction between the factual and the mental, and this Steiner tends to employ interchangeably with that between 'objective' and 'subjective'. Thus, to ask how free a person *feels* is to ask an evaluative question. To ask an evaluative question about freedom is to inquire into a person's subjective mental states. Such an inquiry yields no more than subjective freedom judgements. By contrast, to ask how free a person *is*, is to conduct a factual inquiry. Such an inquiry will yield objective freedom judgements. If one wants reliably objective freedom judgements, one had better adopt a descriptive approach – but the descriptive approach rules out all reference to persons' mental states.

It is important to note that Steiner's response to the problem of the contented slave is stipulative: the problem can equally plausibly be read as casting doubt on the fact / value distinction. It is perfectly plausible to read the problematic of the contented slave as one that precisely queries whether one who genuinely *feels* free can nonetheless coherently be said to *be* unfree.[18] For many, the problem of the contented slave illustrates the intractability, in relation to freedom, of the contrast between the descriptive and the evaluative, the factual and the mental. Unsurprisingly, those who do interpret the problematic of the contented slave in this alternative way have charged Steiner with offering a reductive account of freedom and of free agency. This is sometimes articulated in terms of a charge of behaviourism. One who has pressed this charge is John Gray. According to Gray, himself a supporter of 'impure' negative freedom, descriptive approaches 'constitute a *reductio ad absurdum* of stringent negative libertarianism. For, in leaving us with no way of characterising freedom except in the physicalistic language of unimpeded behaviours, this approach ignores the vital truth that the subject matter of freedom is action rather than behaviour.'[19] For Gray, *actions* are categorically distinct from *behaviour*. Whilst actions do share a physicalist component with the latter, they also include normative rationality requirements: 'an agent should have a reason for what he does'.[20]

For Gray, the fact that the subject matter of freedom judgements is actions rather than behaviour, and the further fact that actions are susceptible to justification by reason, introduces an ineliminably normative dimension into freedom analyses. When judging a person's actions, we necessarily assume certain rational capacities on their part. We assume that the agent had reasons for their action – reasons of which they are in some sense cognizant, and with reference to which they can justify their action. Importantly, for Gray a person's reasons for action can be either good or bad: the normative dimension which Gray has in mind is akin to what I referred to above as

Kant's normative formalism. Gray is not concerned with particular agents' thick evaluative judgements regarding the goodness or rightness or desirability of this or that particular (reasons for) action – what Steiner calls the 'eligibility' of actions. Gray's evaluative dimension is more formal and pertains to a general expectation, which he assumes all agents share, that others are able to give reasons for their actions – that they can respond to the normative demand for justification. Yet a purely descriptive approach such as Steiner's is unable by definition to accommodate the normative, reason-giving dimension which, on Gray's account, is essential to our understanding of what it means to act. This is why it is incapable, according to Gray, of distinguishing between deliberate action and non-deliberate behaviour.

Steiner's response to this charge is puzzling. He assumes that those who press it share his view of actions as a subset of behaviours: 'The behaviourism charge appears to rest on the unquestionably correct claim that actions are only a subset of behaviours.' Steiner adds that 'the usual distinction between behaviours which are also actions and those which are not is that the former satisfy some motivational condition'.[21] He takes Gray to be 'representative' of this position. Yet although Gray concedes that actions include a physical component, he neither treats actions as a subset of behaviours nor refers to a 'motivational condition' in relation to actions. Gray claims that actions are categorically distinct from behaviours, in that actions must satisfy a general rationality requirement: he does not mention motivational conditions.

Steiner's next move is even more curious. He rejects the behaviourism charge as irrelevant, saying that this charge *would* be justified 'if the proper subject of [freedom] judgements was limited, as Gray suggests, to only those behaviours in which persons actually do have a reason to engage'. But limiting the inquiry in this way would be mistaken, for

our freedom judgements are equally concerned with those behaviours in which persons do not, but could, have a reason to engage. I could, though I don't, have a reason to go to the theatre. Yet I am perfectly describable as 'free' or, if prevented, 'unfree' to do so. Our freedom judgements are concerned, that is, with conceivable actions and not just with their subset of actual ones. And since any piece of behaviour is one in which someone could conceivably have a reason to engage – one which is a conceivable action – the pure negative conception construes the prevention or non-prevention of any behaviour as an instance of unfreedom or freedom.[22]

Steiner slides back and forth between 'conceivable' and 'possible' behaviour (and action). Since the proper opposite of an actual action is a possible one, I shall talk of possible behaviour / action rather than of 'conceivable' ones. Although Steiner believes actual actions to be a subset of possible pieces of *behaviour* (rather than, as seems more natural, possible *actions*), he concedes that the distinguishing mark of an action is that it is responsive to a person's reasons for acting. Of course, this is not really what Gray is saying: Gray's claim is that the concept of an action in general invokes the idea of a reason-giving capacity on the part of agents – his concern is not with this or that reason which agents may or may not adduce in support of a particular action. This difference turns out to be of some importance.

As we saw at the outset, Steiner is interested in including in his freedom measurements not only the actual actions that agents perform but also those they could but do not perform – indeed, do not even consider performing. This is why he wants to distinguish between possible pieces of behaviour and actual actions. Possible pieces of behaviours are things that an agent would not be physically prevented by others from doing if they were to take themselves to have a reason to do them: things that they would be unpreventedly free to do even though, having no reason to do them, they don't do. Steiner wants to include possible pieces of behaviour thus conceived in his freedom computations. The underlying thought is plausible: typically, agents are unpreventedly free to do more things than they actually do. Although computing these possible but non-actualized activities is not unproblematic technically,[23] Gray would surely concede at least the pedestrian version of this claim. For example, I am free to go running, swimming and cycling (all at different times), although I actually only go running. Steiner wants to compute under my freedom measurement all three of these possible things that I am unpreventedly free to do, not just the one

I actually do. However, Steiner's terminology further implies that whilst my actually going running shows that I take myself to have reason to do so, thus qualifying as an action, my failure to go either swimming or cycling shows that I do not take myself to have reason to do either of those things, which is why swimming and cycling remain possible pieces of behaviour for me. This is surely wrong: I need not actually go swimming in order to take myself to have a reason for going swimming. I may well take myself to have a reason to go swimming (and judge myself to be unpreventedly free to do so), even though I do not go. One can take oneself to have a reason to do many things one could do but does not do. The fact that one does not do them does not show that one does not take oneself to have a reason to do them. If that is right, the difference between possible pieces of behaviour and actual actions cannot be that only the latter are reason-sensitive. But if possible behaviours are just as reason-sensitive as actual actions, the justification for distinguishing between behaviour and action on those grounds disappears. We might as well simply distinguish between possible actions and actual ones: what distinguishes possible actions from actual ones is not the fact that one has reason to do the latter but not the former, but the fact that one does not actualize the former. It remains open to Steiner to compute possible actions rather than merely actual ones, treating the latter as a subset of the former. The problem is that in so far as possible actions are no less reason-sensitive than actual ones, both types seem to include reference to a general reason-giving capacity of the sort Gray had in mind, undermining Steiner's claims to pure descriptivism.

Clearly, the real disagreement between Steiner and Gray has nothing to do with a semantic dispute over actions versus behaviour. Their real disagreement is over whether or not a person's formal reason-giving capacities in relation to possible and actual actions makes a difference to how free we can judge them to be. Let's abandon talk about action and behaviour and consider, instead, the idea of an option. Steiner wants to say that persons can have options without realizing that they have them, and that, counting these non-recognized options on their behalf, persons can be shown to be freer than they know themselves to be. Gray resists this view.

Recall once more the problem of the contented slave. On Steiner's reading, the slave is objectively unfree, although he fails, subjectively, to appreciate this. More generally, a person may have a range of options available to them yet fail to be cognizant of this fact. Where an option is in fact available to a person who fails to be cognizant of this state of affairs, is that person free or unfree with regard to that option? Consider the following example. A young single mother of three who did not complete her education and who is disgruntled and bored doing nothing but looking after her children finds a letter from the relevant government agency on the doormat of her social housing flat informing her of a new scheme for single mothers wanting to return to work. They will be able to enter conveniently local college education programmes and will be presented, upon enrolment, with childcare vouchers to pay for the necessary hours of child care; they will also be given a list of available child-minders in the local area who have been signed up by the government to this programme. Initially believing the official-looking envelope to contain another 'final' payment demand, the harassed mother scans its contents whilst forcing the pushchair with her screaming two-year-old through the door, dragging the bickering four-year-old behind her in order to embark on her daily round of shopping (thankfully, the seven-year-old is at school). On the way down in the lift she discards the letter, believing it to be of no relevance to her.

Was this person free to enrol on the college course or wasn't she? Was this an option for her? What does it require for something to be an option for one? Is it sufficient for an objective state of affairs to obtain, or is a person's recognition of the given state of affairs as relevant to their situation a further necessary condition for that state of affairs to count as an option for that person? It seems to me that on Steiner's account the mere availability of the government programme renders the woman freer than she was prior to the availability of that programme. Whether she knows it or not, enrolling at college and availing herself of government-funded child care is now a possible course of action for her. Hence, when ascertaining the extent of this woman's freedom, we should include this objectively available course of action in our assessment of how free she is. This woman is freer than she knows herself to be.

Steiner is right to suggest that persons can be mistaken about the extent of the options available to them, and thus about the extent of their freedom. A person can complain that they lack relevant options whilst in fact possessing them. But even if one does believe that such errors of judgement show that a person's subjective evaluation of their situation makes no difference to how free they are in fact, it does not follow that *no one*'s judgement of that person's situation is relevant to determining how free that person is. When no one judges an option to be available to a person, then, arguably, that option is simply not available to that person: all that remain are possible states of affairs that are unbeknown as options to anyone. Assume that we each can, in fact, spread our arms, wriggle the tips of our fingers, and fly to the moon: we just none of us know this. Is flying to the moon an option for us?

Options have to be recognized as such by *someone*, even if they need not always be recognized by the person for whom they are judged to be an option. The harassed mother arguably *is* mistaken in her belief that the government pro-gramme is irrelevant to her situation: she arguably *is* freer than she believes herself to be. But our unswerving commit-ment to this view is the product of *our* evaluative judgement *on her behalf* concerning the relevance to her of the govern-ment programme. We judge there to be a relevant connection between the content of the government letter and her per-sonal circumstances – a connection that leads us to conclude that the woman has been given an option which for some reason she has failed to recognize as such. Perhaps, if one were to talk to the woman – if one were to point out to her the connection between the content of the letter and her personal circumstances – she would change her mind and judge the letter to be of relevance to her situation after all. She might still fail to enrol in the programme. Yet once the woman recognizes that the government programme is of relevance to persons in her kind of situation, once she recog-nizes that she may have reason to take it up, then even if she eventually fails to act on it, it can be said to be an option *for her*. If, on the other hand, after extended discussion with her about her situation and the general aims of the government programme, the woman simply draws a blank – failing to appreciate the ways in which the government letter pertains to her situation – my inclination would be to say, not that she is free but doesn't know it, but that she might be lacking certain evaluative capacities possession of which are a prerequisite to the attribution to her of the capacity for freedom.

The upshot of this discussion is twofold. First, the idea of an 'objective freedom judgement' makes no sense if it is meant to exclude reference to any evaluative dimension at all. No judgement is non-evaluative: to judge *is* to evaluate. When Steiner makes objective freedom judgements, he issues evaluative propositions about the relevance of certain states of affairs to certain persons. Second, Steiner's conception of 'evaluative approaches' to freedom is overly narrow. When Steiner contrasts descriptive with evaluative, factual with mental, objective with subjective, he has in mind persons' subjective evaluative attitudes – attitudes that respond to persons' subjective perceptions of the desirability, goodness or rightness of their actions. Even if Steiner is justified in counselling exclusion of such subjective evaluative attitudes, this does not in itself warrant the exclusion of reference to persons' formal reason-giving capacities in relation to their freedom capacity. This, it seems to me, was Gray's basic point: if we want to say of those who have no capacity at all for the rational comprehension of what they are doing when they are doing it, and why, that they are nonetheless free to do it, we may end up as fully paid-up Hobbesians about negative freedom. But it then becomes difficult to accept why persons should be ruled in, but falling rocks ruled out, by any freedom computations we might care to engage in.

IV. Freedom as Possession: Physical or Normative?

The preceding section concluded that Steiner's distinction between descriptive and evaluative approaches is overly narrow: Steiner fails to differentiate between formal evaluative (normative) capacities and subjective evaluative attitudes. He tends to assume that all evaluative approaches to freedom will make a person's subjectively perceived goodness, etc. of their actions a function of that person's freedom. However, evaluative approaches to freedom need not be built upon persons' subjective evaluative attitudes. When Gray talks of an ineliminably normative dimension in relation to freedom judgements, he has in mind more general reason-giving capacities: his claim is that in predicating freedom of a person, we unavoidably predicate minimal normative rationality of that person. We expect agents to be able to give reasons for their actions, reasons that render their doings intelligible as (free) actions.

Recall the sketch of Kant's account of external freedom in section II. For Kant, the relation of external freedom between two or more agents specifies a reciprocal relation of deliberate non-interference with one another's power of choice. Kant abstracts from agents' particular reasons for non-interference, but nonetheless conceives of non-interference as specifying a non-physical, reason-governed relation between free persons. Given his debt to Kant, once one distinguishes formal normative capacities from subjective evaluative attitudes, might Steiner be persuaded to admit the former even whilst continuing to reject the latter? Not on the face of it. For Kant, as for Berlin and Nozick, a person's coercive threats against another's power of choice do count as freedom preventions: indeed, the state's coercive threat of sanctions constitutes for Kant the paradigm 'prevention' of a person's interference with another's freedom.[24] By contrast, Steiner is adamant that being the recipient of another's coercive threats does not render one unfree. Threats are not physical preventions, hence are not unfreedoms. One may or may not find persuasive Steiner's position concerning threats – the crucial question here is simply whether Steiner is in fact able to remain within the stringently physicalist parameters he sets himself. Can Steiner avoid the objection that he backslides into a normative formalism of the kind at work in Kant's account and independently intimated in Gray's criticisms of pure negative freedom?

I strongly suspect that, in the end, he cannot. In the course of setting out and developing his freedom theory, Steiner repeatedly violates his physicalist strictures. We encountered the first such violation very early on. 'Persons are free to do what they actually do,' said Steiner, adding that 'they're also free to do what they don't do and would never consider doing.' As I argued in the preceding section, such references to possible but non-actualized options presupposes an implicit reference to *someone's* evaluative capacities: where an option remains wholly unrecognized as such by anyone, it cannot be an option. A second violation of physicalist strictures occurs at the point at which Steiner moves from his characterization of freedom as physical non-prevention to the claim that 'freedom is the possession of things', and from there to freedom as a property right. What kind of 'possession' does Steiner have in mind? Is he referring to mere physical possession, or is he presupposing a rather more demanding kind of possession?

Again, consider Kant, who has clearly influenced Steiner's property argument, but who distinguishes between empirical and intelligible possession. Empirical possession is possession of an object in the sense of physically holding it. Intelligible possession is possession of an object without physically holding it. For example, I empirically possess an apple that I hold in my hand, but I possess the apple intelligibly when I can put it on the table over there, walk away from it, and still claim it as mine. According to Kant, the hallmark of a person's property right in an external object is their intelligible possession of the object, not their empirical possession of it. Intelligible possession specifies a three-way normative relation between owner, object and all others who acknowledge the object as belonging to its owner. My property right in the apple on the table is a function not of my physical control over it but of others' acknowledgement of it as mine.

This Kantian idea of intelligible possession does not fit Steiner's descriptive framework. Steiner should confine himself to what Kant calls empirical possession.[25] If freedom is mere physical non-prevention, and one person's physical non-prevention is equivalent to another's possession, the possession in question must be physical possession. And indeed, for some freedom instances mere physical possession may be sufficient. Thus, when our traveller is free to walk down the road he is in (temporary) physical possession of each of the individual bits of road successively occupied by his body: in this sense, persons who are free to do the things they actually do are in (temporary) physical possession of all the physical components necessary to doing those things. However, as we have seen, Steiner is interested not only in the acts that persons actually perform, but also in actions they *could* perform. Steiner accordingly talks not only of actual possession but also of subjunctive possession: 'statements about the freedom or unfreedom of a person to do a particular action are construable as affirmative or negative claims about that person's actual or subjunctive possession of that action's physical components'.[26] In contrast to actual possession, subjunctive possession refers to the things which a person *would* physically possess if they were to do the correspondingly possible action. Subjunctive possession thus refers to *anticipated* physical possession of requisite action components.

Imagine person P doing action X at time t_1. When P does X at t_1 they are in actual physical possession of the physical components of X. Now imagine P at t_1 considering doing X at time t_2. When at t_1 P considers doing X at t_2, P must be assuming *at* t_1 that, *were* P to do X at t_2, P *would*, at t_2, be in physical possession of all relevant X components. Unless P can assume at t_1 that they would physically possess all relevant X components at t_2, doing X at t_2 is not an option for P at t_1. But if P can assume this at t_1, P must be in some kind of possession of X components at t_1. The possession in question cannot be physical possession, since P is not yet actually doing X. At t_1, P must be in possession of X components in some other way. Steiner has a word for it: at t_1 P is in *subjunctive* possession of X components. At t_1 P already (assumes that they) non-physically possess all of the physical X components in such a way that it is within P's capacity at t_1 to do X at t_2. Subjunctive possession is (possibly uncertain) non-physical possession at t_1 of X components to be physically actualized at t_2. Subjunctive possession looks like a species of Kantian intelligible possession. It exceeds the framework of a merely descriptive account of freedom rights.

V. Pure Negative Freedom Evaluated

In the last two sections I tried to show that Steiner's aspiration to provide a *purely* descriptive approach to negative freedom fails. In section III I argued that the notion of an option must include reference to *someone*'s evaluative capacities to recognize a (possible) state of affairs as an option for a person.

In section IV I argued that Steiner's appeal to subjunctive possession in connection with his account of freedom rights as property rights pushes him beyond his physicalist framework in making reference to a non-physicalist form of external possession. Both times my aim was to suggest that the inclusion of some formally normative presuppositions seems in the end inescapable – though this falls short of an inclusion of subjective evaluative attitudes and judgements.

More generally, Steiner's basic premiss – his claim that we each have an equal natural right to freedom – seems to me very difficult to make sense of purely descriptively. Neither the idea of freedom nor the concept of a right seems to me capable of being rendered intelligible in this way. We saw in chapter 3 that Nozick's critics have charged him with offering a 'moralized definition of freedom' – a charge which, read in a certain way, implies the possibility of a normatively neutral account of freedom. Nozick is particularly susceptible to this charge given the strong interrelation, in his account, between freedom and rights. When his critics complain of Nozick's moralized definition of freedom, they usually have in mind his supposedly rights-based definition of freedom. Against this twofold objection I argued that Nozick's account of freedom is not rights-based: instead, his account of rights is freedom-based. But rights-based or not, Nozick's conception of freedom is moral: it attributes overriding moral significance to our purported status as beings possessed of originative value.

In Steiner, too, much is made of the presumed close normative connection between freedom and rights: the difference is that Steiner relies on a metaphysically far sparser account of that connection than one finds in Nozick. To see this, it may help to draw attention to a thus far unmentioned early source of influence upon Steiner's work – H. L. H. Hart's famous article, 'Are There Any Natural Rights?'. The opening proposition of Hart's article states, 'if there are any rights at all, it follows that there must be at least one natural right – the natural right to be free'.[27] One way in which to interpret this opening proposition is to say that Hart is inquiring into the necessary conditions of possible systems of positive rights. For systems of positive rights to be possible, Hart appears to be arguing, we must presuppose the natural right to be free. On this interpretation, Hart is not saying that there *is* a natural right to be free: all he is saying that presupposing such a right is a necessary condition of the possibility of actual systems of positive rights. Otherwise put, we design systems of positive rights because we ascribe to ourselves a natural right to be free. But why ascribe such a natural right to be free to ourselves? What is the significance of our so doing? Systems of positive rights assign entitlements and obligations among persons. In so far as such legal systems presuppose the ascription to rights-holders of a natural right to be free, such ascriptions may most plausibly be interpreted in terms of our general capacity to claim entitlements from others and to incur obligations towards others. This view of the natural right to freedom as denoting persons' capacity to claim entitlements and incur obligations tallies with the Kantian relational metaphysics of external freedom sketched at the beginning of the present chapter: according to it, one person's freedom rights are a function of others' acknowledged freedom obligations towards that person.

Ultimately, Steiner is interested not in freedom, but in rights. More specifically, he is interested in a set of compossible rights: rights that are simultaneously exercisable by different persons. Compossible rights are property rights. Property rights assign exclusive possessions to persons: they constitute, in Steiner's theory, exclusive possession of free action space. This is the descriptive part of Steiner's conception of negative freedom. But why be interested in rights at all – compossible or otherwise? Here, I believe, Steiner ultimately follows Hart: we are interested in rights to the extent to which we suppose ourselves free. Do we suppose ourselves free merely in the descriptive sense? Hart thinks not – he thinks that we suppose ourselves free in so far as we suppose ourselves capable of claiming entitlements and incurring obligations. Something like this thought, I want to suggest, constitutes the non-descriptive core of Steiner's account of freedom: Steiner wants to come up with a purely descriptive account of freedom because he wants to be able to assign determinate entitlements and obligations. Ultimately, it is his non-descriptive freedom commitments which seem to me to drive his search for a descriptive account of freedom as a distributive good.

5

Ronald Dworkin: Liberty as an Aspect of Equality

I. Introduction: Between Negative and Positive Freedom

In 'The Place of Liberty', Dworkin says, 'I mean by liberty what is sometimes called negative liberty – freedom from legal constraint.' Dworkin, it may seem, could hardly be more specific: not only does he tell us that he is interested in *negative* liberty, he also goes on to specify exactly what he means by it – that is, non-interference by the law. If by 'liberty' Dworkin so obviously means negative liberty, why cast him as a proponent of a version of positive freedom? Dworkin also says, on the same page, that he is 'interested not in liberty generally, but only in the connection between liberty and distributional equality'. And a little later he asserts that 'liberty [is] an aspect of equality, rather than, as it is often thought to be, an independent political ideal potentially in conflict with it'.[1] If Dworkin does indeed think of liberty in negative terms, he has an unusual interpretation of it – one which sees it as harmonious with substantive equality rather than as in potential conflict with it, as traditional libertarian proponents of negative liberty tend to believe.[2]

One reason for counting Dworkin as a (part-) advocate of positive liberal freedom is this fact that he conceives of negative liberty not as an independent value but as 'an aspect' of a certain conception of substantive equality. This in itself is unusual. Even more unusual is Dworkin's highly original articulation of substantive equality. According to Dworkin, and in contrast to more standard welfarist accounts of which he is critical, *liberal* equality does not treat all people in exactly the same way. Instead, it treats them differently. Liberal equality shows respect and concern for persons' individuality: it emphasizes not uniformity of treatment but uniqueness of person. Dworkin's conception of liberal equality is premissed on a strong moral ideal of individual independence, whose closest historical precursor is John Stuart Mill's version of the general thesis of individual self-development that Berlin associates with the positive tradition.

Mill is best known for his uncompromising defence, in *On Liberty*, of individual freedom of thought and speech as among the most fundamental of negative liberty rights. Apart from claims about its contribution to general social utility, Mill's most important arguments on behalf of free speech derive from the idea of individual self-development. According to Mill, being left free from interference by government and the moral majority to say what one thinks enhances a person's capacity to judge for themselves. This in turn enhances a person's capacity to lead their life by the lights of their own judgements about what is good for them. Negative liberty is of importance, according to Mill, in so far as it encourages individuals to become independent in thought and action. Becoming independent in thought and action – achieving individuality – is the *telos*, or end, of man as a progressive being.[3]

It is Mill's ideal of individual self-development and his attendant distinction between lower pleasures and higher pleasures (though not between a lower and a higher self!) that induced Berlin, despite Mill's advocacy of negative liberty, to cast him as having one foot in the positive camp. Something similar may be said of Dworkin. Dworkin's defence of negative liberty – absence of legal constraints – is predicated on a strong commitment to what he calls the ideal of ethical individualism. According to this ideal, individuals ought to be left free to discover for themselves what the best life is for them. For both Mill and Dworkin, negative liberty is of importance not as an end in itself, but because of the kind of individual self-development it makes possible.[4] Although neither Mill nor Dworkin expressly invoke the term, Millian independence most closely represents that normative ideal which contemporary liberals have in mind when they refer to the value of individual autonomy. For most contemporary liberals, individual autonomy is synonymous with Mill's ideal of deciding for oneself, independently of others' meddling advice, what the good life is for one.[5] Here it needs be borne in mind that, although it does form part of the positive tradition, Millian individual autonomy is very different from – indeed, is in many ways antithetical to – Kant's account of moral autonomy understood in terms of the will's restraint of subjectively given desires and submission under an objectively valid moral law. While Millian autonomy values individual self-expression and individuals' pursuit of their own conceptions of the good, Kantian autonomy demands abstraction from personal aims and desires and the will's free submission instead under the moral law. It is important not to conflate Millian personal autonomy with Kantian moral autonomy, and equally important to emphasize that Dworkin's debts to the positive tradition are squarely to Mill, not to either Kant or post-Kantian strands of that tradition.

There is, however, an additional sense in which Dworkin can be associated with aspects of the more recent *restatement* of positive freedom made possible through the work of Gerald MacCallum. Mill partakes of the positive tradition on account of his emphasis on individual self-development. Nonetheless, he is in many ways more usually regarded as an advocate of negative freedom. And indeed, for Mill, the absence of legal constraints is the only type of direct government (in)action required to ensure individuals' negative freedom. A person's negative freedom, even though defended by Mill for positive reasons, is secured through government's non-interference with that person's self-regarding judgements and actions. As we saw in chapter 2, this view of governmental non-interference as a sufficient condition for ensuring a person's enjoyment of their negative freedom is rejected by MacCallum in his freedom analysis. According to MacCallum, it is not sufficient to say of a person that they are free to do Z merely in virtue of their being subject to no legal constraints against doing Z. A person must be in a position to make effective use of the absence of legal constraints against doing Z. We saw how, as a result of deploying this criticism of negative freedom, MacCallum succeeded in shifting Berlin's focus upon the positive tradition in terms of self-development concerns to egalitarian-inspired distributive concerns: governments have a positive obligation to ensure that individuals are in a position effectively to avail themselves of legally guaranteed negative liberties.

Unlike MacCallum, Dworkin does not argue that governments have a direct responsibility to enable individuals to be free by supplying them with relevant goods and services. MacCallum's view is premissed on an underlying welfarist conception of distributive equality which Dworkin explicitly rejects. According to Dworkin, a liberal distributive scheme – that is, one which does respect individuals' capacity for personal autonomy – should be so designed as to allow individuals themselves to decide what sort of resources best further their pursuit of their own particular conception of the good life. In consequence, and as we shall see in more detail below, where as MacCallum emphasizes *governments*' responsibilities to provide the right kind of freedom conditions, Dworkin's makes much of the notion of *individual* responsibility for choice within the social distributive context.

In sum, and despite his official statements of interest in 'what is sometimes called negative liberty', when that interest is considered in the context of Dworkin's wider moral and political commitments, his account of the place of negative liberty within that context leaves him closer to certain aspects of the positive tradition than some of his freedom statements, taken in isolation, might seem to suggest. That said, it must be acknowledged that Dworkin does not see himself as an advocate of positive freedom. Instead, he claims to be offering a distinctive philosophical re-articulation of the liberal idea of freedom which takes its cue from what Dworkin believes to be the actual value commitments of citizens in contemporary liberal societies, and which he thinks well placed to overcome the negative / positive distinction. Again, therefore, Dworkin resembles MacCallum in his search for a more unitary, less divisive understanding of liberal freedom. Yet, in contrast to MacCallum's method of conceptual analysis, Dworkin engages in substantive moral and political argument: his principal aim is to revitalize moral and political appreciation of the idea of liberal freedom by re-articulating it in a novel, intuitively plausible and morally attractive manner.

In the remainder of this chapter I shall begin with an outline of Dworkin's ethical individualism, including some discussion of his related distributive theory known as 'equality of resources'. Following this, section III contrasts Dworkin's Millian brand of liberal individualism with Nozick's libertarian individualism, contesting some recent critics' claim that these two forms of individualism are substantially of a kind. Section IV, finally, evaluates Dworkin's equality-based freedom conception from the perspective of the positive tradition and returns, in that context, to some of the criticisms voiced by Berlin against that tradition. Before proceeding, one further note. In general I have treated the terms 'liberty' and 'freedom' interchangeably in this book. While I do believe that the two terms carry somewhat different connotations, these are difficult to spell out and adhere to systematically in a comparative analysis of the sort attempted in this book. In the present case, Dworkin's tendency to slide between a negative conception of freedom as absence of legal constraints and a positive freedom account in terms of individual independence can make it difficult to keep a grip on what sort of freedom he is talking about at different stages in his argument. In an effort to distinguish between them, I shall, in this chapter, reserve the term 'liberty' for negative freedom as defined by Dworkin, using 'freedom' in a more inclusive sense – that is, a sense which, together with absence of legal constraints, includes a concern with and advocacy of personal autonomy.

II. Ethical Individualism Outlined

II. 1. Dworkin's general philosophical method

In contrast to established views regarding the perennial need to balance freedom and equality as two equally important yet conflicting liberal values, Dworkin believes a harmonious approach to them to be possible. Dworkin sharply disagrees with Berlin's assessment of liberalism as not only quintessentially value-pluralistic, but as additionally characterized by deep and irreconcilable value conflicts. According to Berlin, we cannot generally attain all of what is of important to us, either individually or as a society. Perhaps value conflict results from feasibility constraints; perhaps it goes deeper, having to do with the intrinsic nature of the individual values in question. Either way, and while a person may well value X, Y and Z independently, it does not follow that X, Y and Z are compossibly realizable. People must frequently choose between competing values; frequently, the choice of X involves the requirement to forgo Z. Recall Berlin's declaration that 'everything is what it is'. Liberty is liberty: not equality, not justice, not democracy. Liberty may well conflict with equality, justice or democracy. When it does, one will have to choose between liberty and any of these other values. This is cause for regret: nonetheless, one must face up to the fact of a necessary choice between, say, liberty and equality, and must not pretend things to be otherwise. One must not redescribe liberty in terms of equality, such that one ends up saying that no sacrifice of liberty is 'really' involved. To embark on such philosophical redescription is to fail, in a deep sense, to acknowledge the limits of human choice and, consequently, to court political disaster.

Dworkin has little time for Berlin's almost tragic vision of liberal political morality. He is an anti-essentialist about value. According to him, it is not the case that liberty is what it is and equality is what it is, and that when it turns out that the two conflict, there is nothing we can do about it. The substantive content of values is not fixed metaphysically. Instead, values are *abstract* normative ideals that are subject to interpretation by us.[6] Liberty is not what it is: it is what we make of it. The same goes for equality: 'Do liberty and equality, considered as abstract values, conflict in some way that explains why a political community might find itself not merely uncertain about what to do but certain that it must do wrong whatever it does? That depends on what we mean by liberty and equality: it depends on how we conceive these abstract values.'[7] We can, of course, interpret liberty and equality in such a way that they do come out as conflicting. But these are 'hopeless accounts of liberty and equality'[8] that leave us in a self-made moral quandary. Yet why should we condemn ourselves to doing wrong whatever we do, when we can perfectly well do much better than that? To cast ourselves as caught between two conflicting liberal values is to indulge in metaphysical theatrics: and that, too, is to court political disaster!

According to Dworkin, in so far as we *are* committed to freedom and equality as liberalism's two fundamental moral values, it behoves us to develop a harmonious, non-conflictual interpretation of them that understands both as but an aspect of a more general liberal ideal. That more general ideal is what Dworkin calls 'ethical individualism'. Ethical individualism is a distinctly liberal ideal of the good life which Dworkin believes has as a matter of fact come to be so widely embraced among liberals that none seriously doubts its moral and political import: 'I believe that we are now united in accepting the principles [of ethical individualism]: government must act to make the lives of those it governs better lives, and it must show equal concern for the lives of each.'⁹ Methodologically, Dworkin treats our (putative) assessment of the attractiveness of ethical individualism as decisive. Its attractiveness gives us *sufficient* reason to construct an ideal theory of liberal political morality which takes ethical individualism as its central value and arranges social and political institutions accordingly. Dworkin acknowledges no antecedent metaphysical or empirical constraints apart from the attractiveness of ethical individualism to us. He concedes that when we turn from ideal theory 'back towards the real world'¹⁰ we will encounter constraints of implementation: empirically, we may well be able only to *approximate* our ideal moral world. Nonetheless, at the level of normative theorizing, Dworkin is a thoroughgoing humanist, who might well subscribe to the heady 1933 humanist manifesto, signed by John Dewey among others, according to which 'man is at last becoming aware that he alone is responsible for the realization of the world of his dreams, that he has within himself the power for its achievement'.¹¹

II. 2. The principles of ethical individualism

Dworkin analyses the ideal of ethical individualism into what he claims are its two component principles. First, there is the principle of equal value. According to this principle, 'it is intrinsically, objectively, and equally important that human beings lead successful lives; important that once any human life has begun it flourishes rather than founders, and, above all, that it not be wasted'.[12] Each individual *life* is of equal value: far from merely recognizing the bare fact of humans' natural equality, as Hobbes does, or respecting persons' legal equality as natural rights-holders, as Locke counsels, Dworkin exhorts us to acknowledge the moral importance to each person of how their particular life goes in terms of their pursuit of their personal ambitions and projects. As a society, we are to ensure that each person has an equal opportunity to pursue what is of personal moral importance to them, without prejudging any particular forms of the good life as intrinsically more worthy of respect and concern than others.

The second principle of ethical individualism 'declares the connection between you and your life a special one'. This second principle

> insists that this special relationship is best understood as one of special responsibility, that living is an assignment we can execute well or badly. The assignment includes an intellectual challenge: to live out a conception of what makes a life successful, that is personal, in the sense that the agent has embraced it, rather than political in the sense that it has been thrust upon him. Living well, on this view, requires both personal commitment and a social environment in which that commitment is encouraged and respected.[13]

We owe it to ourselves to make something of this life of ours: to take charge of it, to develop our talents, to strive to succeed in our projects. There is the requirement of authenticity: the life we lead must be self-chosen, not 'thrust upon us' by some external authority. Connected with this is the requirement of responsibility for choice: whilst we should be allowed to reap the rewards of our good choices, we should equally expect to pay the price of our bad choices. We should not foist the costs of our bad choices on others, including society in general.

Ethical individualism neatly dovetails Dworkin's equality conception with his view of the value of freedom understood in terms of the idea of individual independence. Liberal equality, which rejects uniformity of treatment, is premised on a view of individuals as capable of such independence: and development of this capacity is each person's special responsibility. On the one hand, others ought to respect us as equals: as distinctive persons with our own lives to lead. On the other hand, they cannot do so unless we each make the effort to develop our individuality. Whilst others ought to be concerned that we flourish, we each have the responsibility to lead a life that we can consider worth living. Note Dworkin's contention that living well requires *both* personal commitment *and* an appropriate social environment. Neither component of ethical individualism can make up for the absence of the other. A life in a socially non-conducive environment is unlikely to have much opportunity to flourish: here appeal to the egalitarian principle is designed to remedy the situation. But nor can a life go well if the person whose life it is fails to take charge of it: here the force of the special responsibility principle kicks in.

II. 3. The distributive scheme of ethical individualism

Dworkin insists that once we understand liberty as an aspect of equality of respect in the manner set out by the principles of ethical individualism, we will appreciate that there can be no conflict between freedom and equality. At times Dworkin appears to backtrack a little, such as when he describes equality as the 'sovereign virtue', implying that, if ever there *were* to be a conflict between liberty and equality, it would be one that liberty would lose.[14] Here the implication is that, ultimately, equality matters more than liberty. Despite these assertions, it is difficult to avoid the impression that things may, in fact, be the other way around: that it may be freedom – more specifically, its value understood in terms of personal autonomy – which enjoys priority over equality in Dworkin's scheme. It is true that Dworkin's principle of equal respect and concern is uncontroversially egalitarian in one sense of that term: we should not show more respect and concern for the lives of some than we do for those of others. Perhaps, when he says that in cases of possible conflict equality trumps liberty, Dworkin has in mind liberty narrowly defined as absence from legal constraints. Perhaps his claim is simply that no liberal government should legally underwrite negative liberties for some that would somehow compromise equality of respect and concern for the lives of others: 'the rights to liberty we regard as fundamental are an aspect of distributional equality, and so are automatically protected whenever equality is achieved'.[15] Here 'rights to liberty' refers to legally guaranteed negative liberties, and the claim is that legal enforcement of negative liberty rights helps to sustain the equality of persons. The trouble is that Dworkin's articulation of what it means to treat persons as equals has his more inclusive freedom commitments built into it. As we have seen, to be treated as an equal in Dworkin's distinctive sense of equality is to have the capacity for independence ascribed to one. One who is treated as equal in Dworkin's sense of the term is one who is credited with the capacity for personal autonomy. In so far as his understanding of liberal equality *presupposes* a commitment to the value of personal autonomy, it may be misleading of Dworkin to cast equality as 'sovereign' over freedom.

The suspicion that it may not be equality that trumps freedom – that things may be the other way around – is especially difficult to rid oneself of in the context of Dworkin's distributive theory, dubbed 'equality of resources' by him, but known more generally as 'luck egalitarianism'. Dworkin's contrast between 'equality of welfare' and 'equality of resources' builds on his conviction that respect for liberal equality demands, not uniformity *of* treatment, but difference *in* treatment: 'There is a difference between treating people equally, with respect to one or another commodity or opportunity, and treating them as equals.'[16] Whereas equality of welfare treats people uniformly by distributing the same commodities or opportunities to all irrespective of morally relevant differences between them, equality of resources treats individuals as equals in the sense of allowing a distribution of resources that reflects their chosen commitments to often radically different conceptions of the good life. Dworkin emphasizes that equality of resources 'establishes a strong presumption in favour of freedom of choice'[17] – a presumption that leads him to designate the market as his favoured distributional 'institution': 'the idea of the market must be at the center of any attractive theoretical development of equality of resources'.

If Dworkin's own contrast between equality of resources and equality of welfare highlights his rejection of the idea of distributive equality as requiring uniformity of treatment, the more general denomination 'luck egalitarianism' draws attention to his focus on individual responsibility for choice. The term 'luck egalitarianism' distinguishes Dworkin's liberal egalitarianism from John Rawls's social egalitarianism, whilst nonetheless indicating a degree of continuity with Rawls. Dworkin endorses Rawls's insistence, against welfarism, upon the 'distinctness of persons'.[18] Yet Dworkin also charges Rawls with overlooking the principle of individual responsibility for choice as an important implication of Rawls's moral individualism. According to Dworkin, individuals' responsibility for the choices they make should be computed in any adequate liberal theory of just distribution. In order to accommodate the responsibility principle in his distributive theory, Dworkin distinguishes between two forms of luck – 'option luck' and 'brute luck'.[19] Option luck refers to the outcomes of a person's voluntary choices. Take as an example a person's voluntary decision to invest in the stock market. The outcome of that voluntary decision could be good or bad: the person may increase their financial assets, or they may incur losses. In so far as the decision to invest was undertaken voluntarily, Dworkin thinks, the consequences of that decision, too, are incurred voluntarily. Losing money in consequence of a voluntary decision to invest is as much a piece of bad option luck as gaining money by such action is good option luck. According to luck egalitarianism, while persons ought to be allowed to enjoy the benefits of their good option luck, they ought also to bear the costs of their bad option luck.

Alternatively, a person may suffer brute luck: bad brute luck in particular. A person suffers brute luck when they bear no responsibility for an event the outcome of which adversely affects them. For example, a person who in walking past a building site has a load of bricks fall on them suffers bad brute luck. Assuming that this person took all reasonable precaution in walking past the building site, they are not responsible for their bad brute luck, and society ought to compensate them. More abstract but politically more relevant examples of bad brute luck include being born with certain handicaps, or being born into deprived socioeconomic circumstances: in cases such as these, society owes affected individuals compensation.[20]

Although it is not possible to offer a complete overview of Dworkin's highly abstract distributive theory, it should be clear that luck egalitarianism 'holds that economic inequalities deriving from differences in people's [choices] and ambitions are justifiable in a way that inequalities deriving from differences of external circumstance are not'.[21] Thus stated, it is plausible to read Dworkin's account as offering a sympathetic amendment to Rawlsian egalitarianism – one that rescinds from Rawls's position merely in order to fine-tune it through the incorporation into Rawls' egalitarianism of a notion of individual responsibility for choice. For a long time, Dworkin's luck egalitarianism tended to be read in that spirit. More recently there has been a sea change among some liberal egalitarians, who view Dworkin's emphasis on individual responsibility for choice as amounting to a betrayal of Rawls's more socially minded egalitarianism.[22] In part, this shift in perception was occasioned by a growing appreciation of the indispensability to Dworkin of the market as the appropriate distributional mechanism. A more immediate cause of philosophical dissent lies in Dworkin's dogged insistence upon the responsibility principle in the face of growing reservations about the feasibility of distinguishing, conceptually or morally, between choice and circumstance in the distributive context. Dworkin's unwillingness to abandon his responsibility principle is indicative of the enormous moral significance which he in fact attaches to it. The pre-eminence of the responsibility principle has led to increasingly vociferous suspicions among fellow liberal egalitarians that Dworkin's basic normative commitments may be too close for comfort to libertarianism. The kinds of complaints levelled against Dworkin's responsibility principle in the distributive context are therefore of special interest to an evaluation of his more general freedom conception. Does the responsibility principle reveal Dworkin's ethical individualism to be a hidden form of libertarianism? I shall argue that this is not the case.

III. Ethical Individualism Assessed

Dworkin believes that ethical individualism represents an attractive, widely accepted liberal moral ideal. He thinks its attractiveness sufficient reason to embrace it and working towards its political realization. Unlike Berlin, Dworkin does not labour under what one might call a metaphysics of human limitations – a world-view according to which not everything is up for human choosing. In that sense Dworkin is a more thoroughgoing humanist than any of the thinkers so far examined, with the possible exception of MacCallum. It may be tempting to take his dismissal of antecedently given constraints on normative theorizing as indicative of an (implicitly held) incompatibilist metaphysics of moral and political agency. And indeed, a number of recent egalitarian critics have accused him of being, effectively, a libertarian – metaphysically as well as politically. According to these critics, notwithstanding the egalitarian veneer of ethical individualism, its heart is the principle of individual responsibility for choice. These critics object to Dworkin's contention that individual persons ought not to be compensated for the bad consequences of bad choices voluntarily undertaken. They believe Dworkin's hard-nosed attitude to betray underlying libertarian political commitments – although many also find his obsessive concern with individual responsibility indicative of a kind of Victorian moral high-mindedness not usually associated with libertarianism as a political doctrine.[23]

Some go further. Samuel Scheffler has recently argued not only that luck egalitarianism betrays libertarian traits in the political sense of the term, but also that it is premised on an incompatibilist metaphysics of choice: 'the plausibility of luck-egalitarianism tacitly depends on a libertarian conception of what genuine choice would look like'.[24] Scheffler deems incompatibilism an 'unattractive' and 'implausible' metaphysics of free will, and he implies that what he judges to be the unattractive features of luck egalitarianism are a consequence of an underlying incompatibilist metaphysics. I shall argue that Scheffler is mistaken on this particular count. While I agree with Scheffler that the moralizing overtones of ethical individualism are amongst its least appealing features, I shall suggest that this aspect of ethical individualism is more plausibly related to Dworkin's indebtedness to Millian compatibilism. Here Nozick provides a useful point of contrast with Dworkin: useful, not only because Nozick *is* a libertarian politically and metaphysically, but also because the charge of moralism has been levelled against Nozick as well. I shall argue (1) that in so far as Nozick is an incompatibilist about free will, it is hard to see how Dworkin could be; and (2) that the charge of moralism is in many ways more appropriate in relation to Dworkin's compatibilism than to Nozick's incompatibilism.

III. 1. Dworkin's compatibilism

I said above that Dworkin discards as irrelevant considerations of antecedently given metaphysical constraints; the putative attractiveness of ethical individualism is itself sufficient for constructing a political morality around it. Given this, it may seem odd now to attribute a compatibilist metaphysics to Dworkin. In general, Dworkin may well be a compatibilist about freedom, yet think this fact about his metaphysical freedom beliefs irrelevant in the context of normative political theorizing – a position common among contemporary political philosophers. Alternatively, Dworkin may have *no* view on the metaphysics of freedom; he may be genuinely agnostic with regard to this issue. Neither possibility is relevant now. Whether Dworkin himself is or is not a compatibilist about freedom is not at issue. My aim is merely to argue, against Scheffler, that Dworkin's account of ethical individualism and luck egalitarianism cohere better with a compatibilist metaphysics than with an incompatibilist one.

According to the second principle of ethical individualism, there is a special connection between a person and the life they lead: each person is responsible for leading the life that they in fact lead. Although Dworkin immediately modifies this strong statement of individual responsibility by setting it out alongside the egalitarian principle which requires society to assist persons in their attempts to lead flourishing lives, his emphasis on individual self-development and individual responsibility bears a surface resemblance to Nozick's view of individuals as setters of ends. Recall Nozick's incompatibilist metaphysics of free will, which attributes to persons a capacity for 'reflexively self-subsuming, weight-bestowing decisions'. It is in virtue of this capacity that individuals are originators of value, and it is their capacity for incompatibilist free choice thus conceived which Nozick identifies as the source of persons' moral status as ends. For Nozick, their incompatibilist freedom of choice is a defining feature of individual personhood: this is why violating a person's freedom rights is tantamount to violating their moral status as a person. A second, and in certain respects more radical, implication of Nozick's metaphysics of free will is the idea of persons as having the capacity to create their practical identity *ex nihilo*. Recall Nozick's numerous decisionistic references to individuals' leading their own lives, deciding what is important to them, deciding who, practically, they are going to be. Nozick assumes no antecedents other than the person's capacity for reflexively self-subsuming, weight-bestowing decision making as a condition for free practical self-creation. References to particular talents, character traits, and psychological dispositions are noticeable for their absence. Persons create themselves, practically speaking, through the exercise of mere, sheer power of choice.

Dworkin repudiates both these aspects of Nozickian individualism. He denies that freedom is *constitutive* of personhood. He also denies that persons create their practical identities 'from nothing' – that is, merely on the basis of exercising their incompatibilist power of choice. Both these differences are more naturally associated with corresponding compatibilist commitments. Consider the first objection. In *Taking Rights Seriously (TRS)* Dworkin mounts a strong challenge against what he takes to be the political libertarian's preoccupation with a general right to freedom. Although the general right to liberty is 'a popular and inspiring idea',[25] it has also 'caused more confusion than it has cured'.[26] Properly speaking, 'there exists no general right to liberty at all'.[27] Dworkin is not saying that there are no liberty rights that are worth having. To the contrary, he is an uncompromising defender of classic liberty rights, such as the right to free speech, the right to freedom of conscience, the right to freedom of political association. He merely denies that there is a right to freedom 'in general': and he denies this because he does not believe there to be any such 'thing' as freedom. Dworkin's denial tallies with MacCallum's rejection of Berlin's notion of freedom *simpliciter*. We saw that, for MacCallum, talk about freedom *simpliciter* is nonsensical:

according to freedom as a triadic concept, there are only specific freedoms to do specific things. Dworkin's rejection of a right to liberty 'as such', in the face of his simultaneous endorsement of particular liberty rights, is of a piece with MacCallum's objection to freedom *simpliciter* and his endorsement of innumerable possible individual free actions.

Closely connected to Dworkin's denial of a general right to freedom is his repudiation of what Ian Carter calls 'the independent value of freedom'.[28] Freedom is not valuable in itself: its value is a function of the many other things that it enables us to do. Consider Dworkin's opening declaration of interest in negative liberty and his immediate specification of negative liberty as absence of legal constraints. According to Dworkin, to be negatively free to say what you think is to be free from legal constraints on public speech. Dworkin attaches great moral and political importance to the right to free speech. But this right is important not because of the independent value of freedom, but because of the value of being able freely to speak one's mind unhindered by others. We value liberty rights because of the kind of things these rights allow us to do. We do not value liberty 'itself'.

In the present context, the important point in Dworkin's position regarding the instrumental value of specific liberty rights is that it is not suggestive of a view of freedom as constitutive of personhood. For Dworkin, any plausible account of what it is to be a person need make no reference to their putative metaphysical status as 'free beings' or to their 'being free *simpliciter*'. Liberty violations are not, on Dworkin's understanding of them, direct violations of a person. Such violations are morally repugnant in that they amount to unwarranted interferences with a person's legally permitted actions. Being able to engage in these legally permitted actions is of great importance, moreover, to personal development. Even so, liberty violations are not attacks on personhood. This view of freedom of choice as instrumentally valuable fits a compatibilist metaphysics. It is indicative of a view which embraces Humean freedom as (caused) spontaneity of choice whilst rejecting freedom as indifference of the will. As we saw in earlier chapters, for one who endorses freedom of indifference, talk about freedom *simpliciter is* intelligible: we can think of ourselves as (causally) free whether or not we exercise our capacity for freedom at any particular moment in time. By contrast, one who rejects the general idea of free choice as coherently conceivable apart from particular acts of choice is more likely to embrace Humean freedom of spontaneity, according to which it is particular opportunities to choose between available options, not the capacity for choice *simpliciter*, which are of value. It is misleading of Scheffler to suggest that Dworkin's responsibility thesis 'will seem most plausible if those notions [of choice and responsibility] are given a "libertarian" or "incompatibilist" interpretation, according to which genuinely voluntary choices belong to a different metaphysical category than do other causal factors'.[29] Dworkin never invokes the idea of the will as belonging to a 'different metaphysical category'; nor does luck egalitarianism in general do so. Dworkin's rejection of the idea of freedom *simpliciter*, together with his defence of the non-independent, instrumental value of freedom cohere better with the compatibilist idea of freedom as spontaneity of choice than with the incompatibilist conception of indifference of the will.

III. 2. Dworkin's moralism

Scheffler rightly associates incompatibilism with a commitment to a 'special' metaphysical category of causality; he correctly characterizes incompatibilist conceptions of individual responsibility for choice in causal terms: this characterization does tally with the manner in which Nozick conceives individual responsibility for choice. Compatibilists reject such resort to a special metaphysical category as at best implausible and at worst incoherent. They tend to explain individual responsibility for choice dispositionally rather than causally. A dispositional approach to responsibility attribution arguably also underlies Dworkin's responsibility thesis.

I noted that Dworkin is like Nozick in ascribing to persons the capacity to make something of themselves. Yet he is unlike Nozick in attaching great moral importance to persons' 'getting it right'. Where a person fails to make 'the best' of their life, or fails, at any rate, to try to do so, they are, on Dworkin's account, failing themselves: they are 'wasting' their life. It is in his rejoinder to 'live life well' that many of his critics detect moralizing overtones. It is worth contrasting the charge of moralism levelled at Dworkin with that raised against Nozick. Nozick's critics, recall, decry as a 'moralized conception of freedom' his view that a person is free to do what they have a right to do. Thus stated, the moralism charge is ambivalent between asserting that Nozick operates with a normatively non-neutral conception of freedom and complaining that he is 'moralistic' about the value of freedom. I want to suggest that while Nozick's conception of freedom is indeed normatively non-neutral, he is not a 'moralist' about the value of individual freedom. According to Nozick, when individuals act beyond their freedom rights, the wrong they commit is that of violating *another*'s freedom. Yet so long as a person acts within their freedom rights, Nozick does not judge between good or bad uses of their freedom. A person may make foolish or reckless choices which others may or may not disapprove of and which the person themselves may or may not come to regret having made. However, bad choices are not in any sense deficient exercises of a person's freedom; they are not 'wasted opportunities'. A person is not to be judged the less capable of freedom for having made a bad choice; nor is there a moral expectation that a person learn from the bad choices they have made. We may say that for Nozick the independent value of freedom takes priority over the good or bad value of particular choices. Nozick does expect persons to take (causal) responsibility for their bad choices in the sense of acknowledging the choice as having 'originated' with them. He also assumes that persons will typically have to bear the cost of their bad choices; but if so, this is not because they deserve to do so, but because others are within their rights to choose not to help.

By contrast, Dworkin does counsel distinguishing between deserved and undeserved bad luck, and he does advocate different moral responses to these two kinds of luck. It is this moral high-mindedness which critics like Elizabeth Anderson object to. But such moral high-mindedness is not grounded in an incompatibilist metaphysics. It is more reminiscent of compatibilist attributions of responsibility for character. Consider Mill's position, according to which a person's will is no less subject to causal determination than any other phenomenon in the natural world. Nonetheless, deliberate choice between two or more given options remains possible. Moreover, a person shapes (and reinforces) their character over time by making certain kinds of deliberate choices rather than others. Mill believes that rational reflection can make a difference even on the assumption of the will's causal determination. When confronted, compatibly, with a choice between option A and option B, a person may choose to do A because they prefer to do A even though they rationally understand B to be the morally better choice, and even though, based on that understanding, they know that they could have chosen B instead. We may say that such a person knowingly makes a morally inferior choice in the face of an equally available, morally superior alternative option. In knowingly choosing the morally inferior option, the person may be said to have betrayed something about their character. One might even say that, in choosing morally inferior A over morally superior B the person endorsed and so reinforced some aspect of their character which they could have chosen not to endorse. Over time, a person may repeatedly make choices of a kind that reinforce certain character traits rather than others; in so doing, they acquire a character which they could have chosen not to acquire. It is this character that they can be held morally responsible for having acquired through their choices over time.

I want to suggest that Dworkin's responsibility principle is premissed on something like this dispositional account of responsibility attribution. Part of Dworkin's insistence that persons should bear the costs of their bad choices has to do with encouraging them to make the right kind of choices and to develop themselves in the right kinds of way. The underlying moralism of Dworkin's responsibility principle comes to the fore in his elaboration of the morally good liberal life: 'ethical liberalism assumes that it is important how people live – important that they lead successful or good lives rather than bad or wasted ones'.[30] Dworkin emphasizes that there are no external criteria of what it is for a life to be successful. He distinguishes between the 'impact model' and the 'challenge model' of a successful life, endorsing the latter over the former. According to the impact model, 'the impact of a person's life is the difference his life makes to the objective value in the world'.[31] On this view, the life of a Nobel prize-winning medical scientist who has discovered a cure for AIDS will be deemed more successful than that of a police officer who has managed to prevent a number of crimes; both will be more successful lives than that of the ordinary house-husband who has succeeded 'only' in raising his children.

By contrast, the 'challenge model' of a successful life asks us to think of the execution of our lives 'as having the inherent value of a skilful performance' – as akin to a 'brilliant dive into the pool' the success of which lies simply in the 'skill and elegance' of its execution.[32] It is not easy to set out succinctly what precisely Dworkin means by a successful life's amounting to a 'skilful performance': the underlying thought appears to be that we should not assess how well or badly our life goes compared to that of others, but that we should evaluate it on its own terms. Whatever hand we're dealt, whether we are born into the lap of luxury or faced with unending adversities, we can respond to these challenges either well or badly. We should not compare our lives to those of others in order to gauge the relative success of ours: instead, we should apply internal criteria of assessment to the life which we have been 'assigned' and the responsibility for making a success of which is ours.

As Richard Arneson has shown in some detail, there are considerable difficulties with the challenge model as a plausible model for thinking about a successful life.[33] Here it is important to note a degree of continuity between Dworkin's articulation of what it is to lead a successful life and the Millian dispositional notion of responsibility for character. The connection is especially clear once Dworkin's further distinction between 'volitional interests' and 'critical interests' is taken into account – a distinction which tracks Mill's own distinction between lower and higher pleasures. Mill's distinction reflects his rejection of Jeremy Bentham's hedonistic dictum that 'pushpin is as good as poetry'. Whilst Bentham holds that we should not distinguish between the relative merits of individual particular persons' wants or preferences, Mill strongly believes that some pleasures are more worthy of pursuit than others, and that we owe it to ourselves to pursue the more worthwhile ones. We might, of course, find that we do indeed prefer pushpin – a lower pleasure – to poetry – a higher one; but if we do, we ought to acknowledge that we should not, and ought to try to reverse our preference order. As progressive beings with the capacity for self-development, we should try for the higher pleasures rather than the lower ones.

Dworkin similarly defines a person's 'volitional interests' as referring to the kinds of things they in fact want to have: 'someone's volitional well-being is improved, and just for that reason, when he has or achieves what in fact he wants'.[34] A person may have a volitional interest in sailing well, for example, just because they enjoy sailing and want to excel at it. By contrast, a person's 'critical interests' refer to the things that are of *moral* interest to them: 'having a close relationship with my children, for example, securing some success in my work – these I regard as critical interests because I believe that my life would be a less successful one if I failed to have, or wholly failed to achieve, these goals'.[35] The specific contents of volitional interests on the one hand and critical interests on the other will differ from life to life: depending on their natural endowments and social circumstances, individuals will value different things both volitionally and critically speaking. Moreover, Dworkin believes pursuit and (partial) fulfilment of both a person's volitional interests and their critical interests to be necessary components of a life well lived. Nonetheless, a person's critical interests weigh more heavily in the scales of ethical assessment. One who habitually chooses to favour their volitional interests over their critical interests is 'wasting' their life, is making less of it than they might have done and than the special responsibility principle expects of them.

Dworkin's notion of a life well lived as a life which is adequately responsive to the particular challenges it is confronted with, his distinction between volitional and critical interests, his expectation that a successful life will include a greater proportion of the latter, his judgements that lives are less successful if they contain predominantly the former – all these pronouncements do have the scent of moralism about them, not least when read in conjunction with the rejoinder that persons should bear the costs of their voluntary bad choices and should not turn to society for compensation. One may or may not find Dworkin's position attractive; one may or may not think it a plausible approach to assessing the success of one's life. But whether or not one does, one should not make the mistake of conflating either Dworkin's normative position or its implicit metaphysics with a libertarianism of either kind. Dworkin's ethical individualism is heavily indebted to a conception of individual self-development which one finds in Mill and which is quite foreign to the libertarian political outlook, which emphasizes choice and causal responsibility for choice but says nothing at all about the intrinsic moral goodness or badness of any particular choices. Similarly, the emphasis on character development and the related dispositional attribution of responsibility for choice is foreign to incompatibilist, causal responsibility attributions, yet familiar to dispositional compatibilist approaches to responsibility for character formation.

IV. Ethical Individualism and Positive Freedom

If I have dwelt at some length on critics' twofold charges of a hidden libertarianism in Dworkin's approach, this is partly because it is interesting to see how, despite superficial similarities, Dworkin's ethical individualism differs from Nozick's thesis of 'originative value' both normatively and metaphysically. But I have done so also because it seems to me that the current tendency among some of Dworkin's egalitarian critics to decry him as a closet libertarian runs the danger of misdiagnosing the source of what may indeed be problematic about his ethical individualism. In this concluding section I want to suggest that the kinds of moral worries that seem to arise for egalitarians in particular are related (a) to the excessively idealistic nature of ethical individualism, and (b) to the intrusion of ethical considerations into the political, distributive context. Interestingly, both concerns may be seen to echo some of Berlin's worries in relation to the positive freedom tradition.

Initially, recent egalitarian expressions of normative dissent from Dworkin's position seem surprising, given Dworkin's not implausible contention merely to be following the lead of settled public convictions regarding the centrality, within liberal public culture, of ethical individualism as a moral ideal. Dworkin is not alone among liberal philosophers in theorizing the ideal of personal autonomy as central to contemporary liberal political morality. To many current liberal theorists, the

ideal of personal autonomy best articulates the moral significance of liberal freedom. Indeed, many contrast this ethically
richer approach with what they perceive to be the morally
bereft, economically driven, choice-focused analyses of libertarian competitors.[36] It is not implausible to speak of the
revival of a central value within the positive tradition which,
though much maligned in Berlin's analysis, is nonetheless seen
to articulate an ineliminable aspect of the personally emancipatory promise associated with the liberal idea of freedom.
Given all this, why should Dworkin's luck egalitarianism,
centred as it is on the publicly widely endorsed *non-libertarian*
value of personal autonomy, have incurred increasingly
critical responses from among those whom one would otherwise expect to be sympathetically disposed towards that
non-libertarian ideal?

It should be noted that the critics referred to in the previous section do not tend to take issue with Dworkin's ethical
individualism as such: they take issue with the principle of
individual responsibility which is derived from it and which
plays such a decisive role in Dworkin's distributive theory. In
fairness to Dworkin, it should also be noted that the initial
concerns of 'equality of resources' were focused on undercut-
ting public funding for what Dworkin then described as
'champagne tastes' – expensive preferences that individual
persons may develop simply because (in Dworkin's judgement) welfarist distributive theories encourage them to do so.
The distinction between option luck and brute luck was meant
to help discriminate between morally warranted and morally
unwarranted distributive claims: as indicated earlier, standard
social examples of Dworkinian brute luck are being born with
physical or mental impairments, finding oneself in deprived
socio-economic circumstances through no doing of one's own,
suffering discrimination as a result of the prejudices of others.
It is for such cases of brute luck that 'equality of resources'
was intended to claim socially funded compensation, whilst
denying it to those, say, who incur lung cancer as a result of
smoking thirty cigarettes a day while fully cognizant of the
dangers of so doing.

The problem is that, when considered in relation to the 'real
world' of actual liberal societies, it became ever more mani-
fest that those born through no fault of their own into socially

deprived circumstances are often also those who voluntarily smoke thirty cigarettes a day even whilst aware, in some abstract sense of that term, of the dangers of so doing. In other words, it is often the socially less fortunate who 'voluntarily' make bad or risky choices – either from ignorance, or from lack of realistic alternatives, or simply from socially inherited habits. When applied to the real world of social deprivation, 'equality of resources' seems to have the paradoxical outcome that it distributes to the socially deprived with one hand whilst taking from them with the other.

From the perspective of our present concerns, an important implication of these findings at the level of Dworkin's distributive theory is that the ethical ideal which the distributive scheme is based on may not be feasible: it may be *too* idealistic. Again, this concern applies not only to Dworkin's autonomy account. There is the general worry that what liberal philosophers mindful of the ethics of liberalism describe as the value of personal autonomy tends to translate, in many of the social practices of actual liberal societies, into the more or less frantic pursuit of multitudinous small-scale commercial transactions. To put it bluntly: what is described as independence of judgement regarding the good life within liberal philosophical circles is often imperfectly mirrored, in real liberal lives, in little more than the choice, advocated on the commercial channels, between one brand of yoghurt over another. Assessed against the social reality of a substantial section of the populations of liberal societies – those sections which distributive theories are traditionally designed to reach – Dworkin's ethical individualism may simply be too far-fetched. Indeed, one might go further, asking whether the degree of agent control and success required by Dworkin's challenge model is realistically attainable by more than the very few. Perhaps Dworkin is describing the lives of the professional classes: his more concrete examples – sailing well, succeeding in 'one's' work – often seem to suggest this. But even here, the extent of a person's overall control and independence with regard to their life seems exaggerated.

Of course, Dworkin would say that the principles of ethical individualism describe a moral ideal – one which we can aspire towards but will only ever be able to attain in degrees. Clearly, this response has *some* purchase. Even so, some moral ideals are more realistic than others; the worry is that ethical individualism may be one of the less realistic ones. If so, this may have repercussions for the application of Dworkin's distributive theory to real-life contexts. Dworkin holds that the principles of ethical individualism should inform distributive policies: individuals should take responsibility for their lives, and should not be compensated for bad choices voluntarily made. But if the ethical principles informing Dworkin's distributive scheme are particularly unrealistic in relation to those to whose lives the existence of distributive schemes potentially makes the most difference, there is a very real danger that the merit of their claims will end up being measured by criteria that are wholly irrelevant to their actual situation. It is, I believe, this potential danger that critics like Anderson and Scheffler identify in Dworkin's approach. It is, moreover, one that is reminiscent, to some extent, of some of Berlin's criticisms of the position tradition.

Berlin, we saw, charged advocates of the positive tradition with a penchant for appeals to 'the true value' of freedom, and he thought that this tendency made those theories particularly liable to political abuse. Underlying the charge is the classic liberal worry over the introduction of ethical ideals into the realm of politics. The worry is that, when enforced through the unavoidably coercive mechanisms of politics, these ideals can have disastrous consequences for those on the receiving end. It would be misplaced to charge Dworkin with either the blunt assertion of 'ethical truths' or with an enthusiasm for their political enforcement by coercive means: crucially, Dworkin makes his responsibility principle conditional upon widespread public acceptance of the principles of ethical individualism. Where these principles are not widely accepted as a matter of fact, equality of resources simply cannot get off the ground. Nonetheless, the theoretical point holds: Dworkin's ethical individualism intrudes upon the sphere of politics – the sphere of social distribution – in ways in which liberals like Berlin argue ethics should not intrude, given the coercive nature of political enforcement. In this context it is worth noting that Mill himself, from whom Dworkin draws so much inspiration, did not advocate public policy making based on ethical ideals: ironically, in the distributive sphere Mill would more likely have favoured the sort of pragmatic and individually undifferentiated welfarism that Dworkin so vehemently repudiates.

I have suggested that it is possible to read Dworkin as doing what Berlin warns liberals against – making policy recommendations based on purported ethical truths or ideals. This is not what Dworkin thinks of himself as doing: still, there may be a structural overlap between Dworkin's recommendation to pursue ethical individualism by political means and Berlin's diagnosis of a similar if rather more sinister trend within the positive tradition. I argued in chapter 1 that Berlin's charge is overdrawn: that he is too quick to single out the positive tradition in this respect. Moral truth peddling is just as much a pastime among advocates of *negative* freedom, Berlin included. And it would be deeply unfair to accuse Dworkin of 'corrupting' political processes through the inclusion of ethical ideals. Nonetheless, the tendency to over-idealize ethical individualism seems to me to be clearly present in Dworkin's writings. Given the significance of ethical individualism for his distributive theory, and given the unavoidably coercive nature of 'real' politics even in the distributive sphere, such over-idealization should be avoided.

There is a further aspect of Dworkin's ethical liberalism which I want finally to mention, if only briefly. It concerns the manner in which Dworkin conceives of the idea of individual responsibility. When examining MacCallum's partial restatement of positive freedom in chapter 2, I lamented his eclipse of the idea of individual responsibility for freedom and its alternative emphasis on governmental responsibility. Whereas on Rousseau's account freedom is a shared social responsibility that joins citizens together in a common political venture, in MacCallum we tend to end up with individual citizens as more or less passive recipients of government-provided 'freedom benefits'. By contrast, in Dworkin we return to the idea of individual responsibility for freedom. However, the shared structure of that responsibility is largely lost. Dworkin's ethical individualism tends to privatize each person's personal freedom responsibility. He insists that we are each responsible for our own lives. Although this responsibility assignment has distributive repercussions for each one of us, these are experienced, in the first instance, by each of us privately. In the second instance, of course, the privatized nature of Dworkinian freedom responsibilities may encourage the emergence of a social fabric that is in certain respects not unlike the one envisaged for very different reasons by Nozick: a society of sovereign, mutually disinterested liberal ethicists. Dworkin makes some attempt to resist this picture. Our lives go better, he asserts, when we live in a just society. Yet such *ad hoc* attempts at liberal community fail to convince: is Dworkin not simply saying that we have *prudential* reason to take an interest in social justice in so far as doing so will make our *own* lives go better? Possibly, Dworkin's ethical individualism is in fact well suited to the highly fragmented nature of contemporary liberal public culture: it may be genuinely unrealistic to expect individual citizens to take a sustained interest in the idea of freedom as a shared moral and political enterprise. Nonetheless, there are liberal thinkers who believe that the fragmentation of liberal moral and political culture is all too accentuated in mainstream liberal theorizing, and who argue that a firmer commitment to the ideal of personal autonomy as a shared public good is morally desirable as well as politically feasible. One of those thinkers is Joseph Raz, our final subject of inquiry in this book.

6
Joseph Raz: The Social Value of Personal Autonomy

I. Introduction: Raz and Liberal Perfectionism

In one sense the inclusion of Joseph Raz's work on liberal freedom in this book is anomalous. Although an advocate of a particular conception of personal autonomy, Raz's position is related only indirectly to the positive tradition as delimited by Berlin. Raz does not draw on Kant or Hegel – nor, much less, does he appeal to Rousseau. And although he clearly is indebted to John Stuart Mill's writings, even his use of Mill is eclectic. The deeper intellectual influence upon Raz's general philosophical outlook is Aristotle. Raz is associated with what sometimes goes by the name of 'liberal perfectionism' – a philosophical direction within liberalism which emerged in conscientious point of contrast with that of 'liberal neutrality' some twenty years ago. It is in part their endeavour to formulate, against advocates of liberal neutrality, a more substantive, community-oriented conception of liberal morality that led liberal perfectionists to turn to Aristotle's normative naturalism and virtue ethics.

The idea of liberal neutrality expresses the idea of a government's being neutral between divergent possible conceptions of the good life. A liberal government should not favour or enforce by political means any particular conception of the good life. It should not base its policy making on any specific conception of what is good or valuable, for to do so would be to discriminate against some conceptions of the good life in favour of others.[1] Underlying the idea of liberal neutrality are the phenomena of secularization and multiculturalism, both of which have contributed significantly to the emergence of value pluralism within liberal societies. In part for this reason, liberal neutrality is seen as conceptually continuous with liberalism's historical commitment to the principle of toleration. The idea of liberal neutrality is also often thought consonant with both negative and positive freedom conceptions. A negative point in favour of liberal neutrality is the thought that government has no business interfering with individuals' activities, whatever these are, so long as they are legal. A positive point is that liberal neutrality is a condition of individuals being able to discover for themselves what the good life is for them.[2]

Liberal perfectionism grew out of dissatisfaction with the idea of liberal neutrality.[3] Conceptually, liberal perfectionists decried as incoherent the articulation of neutrality as a political value: to *advocate* neutrality is not to be neutral towards the idea. Normatively, perfectionists argued that it is neither possible nor desirable for policy-makers to be morally neutral. Public policies are always premised on *some* conception of what it is desirable or valuable or morally necessary for a society to do or not to do. More generally, perfectionists urged neutralists to recognize and acknowledge liberalism as a relatively determinate political morality, with a fairly specific idea at least of how people should *not* live – in particular, of how they should *not* live-together – and a good idea, therefore, of what general form the rules of social and political engagement should take. The debate has since died down, with concessions from both sides. Neutralists agree that liberal neutrality is to be had, if at all, only in degrees, and perfectionists agree that the scope for value pluralism and toleration is considerably greater in liberal societies than under most alternative political arrangements.

Raz's book, *The Morality of Freedom* (MF), was written at a time when the idea of liberal neutrality was in its ascendancy. It urges a non-neutral understanding of liberal political morality. It does so in a subtle and original manner, and, unsurprisingly, the book has survived the neutrality–perfectionist debate, standing as an important work in contemporary liberal philosophy in its own right. The focus of the present chapter is on Raz's arresting claim that personal autonomy is best understood as a liberal *social* value. This is an unusual approach to the subject, given the virtually unanimous consensus within more mainstream liberalism on a conception of personal autonomy as a distinctly *individual* value that requires assertion and protection against potential incursions by government and society in general. Of course, in decrying personal autonomy as a social value, Raz is not suggesting that it is liberal societies rather than their individual members that have the capacity to pursue and attain personal autonomy.[4] Personal autonomy is seen by Raz as indexed to individuals: only individual persons can be autonomous. Nonetheless, Raz contends that it is not possible for individuals to become personally autonomous outside societies that value personal autonomy socially and whose institutions and practices reflect that fact. Perhaps even more startling is his further contention that just as it is impossible for persons to become autonomous in non-autonomy-valuing societies, so it is likewise difficult for persons to evade the demands of personal autonomy in autonomy-valuing societies. Put simply: just as liberal individuals living in non-liberal societies will find it hard to be autonomous, so non-liberal individuals living in liberal societies will find it hard to be non-autonomous.

Much of the present chapter is taken up with an exploration of this unusual approach to the liberal value of personal autonomy. Although Raz's Aristotelianism places him outside the classic negative / positive debate as outlined by Berlin, he is the foremost contemporary proponent of a liberal perfectionist conception of personal autonomy, which is set out systematically and with a great deal of plausibility. There is, moreover, thematic continuity between Raz's account and aspects of the positive freedom tradition more conventionally conceived. Raz thematizes the connection between autonomy and reason, and his account includes a social perspective upon personal autonomy that is in certain respects closer to the positive tradition than Dworkin's more individualistic approach. There are also interesting tensions between Razian personal autonomy and more standard liberal freedom conceptions. Among the most intriguing is Raz's view of the relation between autonomy and choice: whilst he emphasizes choice as an essential requirement of personal autonomy, he simultaneously downplays its moral significance considered independently of the latter. Given its importance for situating Raz's perfectionist autonomy account, his ambivalent position on the relation between reason and autonomy, on the one hand, and autonomy and choice, on the other, will be the principal topic of evaluation in this chapter's concluding section IV. Before turning to this issue, it is necessary to say more, in section II, about Raz's general neo-Aristotelian method of approach. Section III explores the perfectionist idea of personal autonomy as a social value, considering both the value of autonomy thus conceived and the social conditions of its exercise.

II. Raz's Aristotelianism: Reason and Value

I said that Raz's general philosophical approach constitutes a particular kind of moral perfectionism – an attempt to retrieve Aristotelian virtue ethics for contemporary moral and political thinking. Raz rarely thematizes his Aristotelianism explicitly. There is no discussion of virtue ethics in *MF*; Raz's many other writings on practical reasoning, too, are devoid of extended discussions of Aristotle.[5] Nonetheless, the Aristotelian influence is palpable, especially in Raz's general conception of the relation between reason and value. Here neo-Aristotelians are somewhat handicapped by Aristotle's pre-modern natural teleology. According to the latter, nature in general and everything in nature are organized purposively. Every natural organism, animate or inanimate, strives towards fulfilment of its particular purpose. A tadpole has the purpose, or *telos*, of becoming a frog, an acorn has the *telos* of becoming an oak tree, man has the *telos* of becoming a eudaimon – what one might translate, roughly, as a morally rounded, virtuous, hence contented and fulfilled person. Of course, having a *telos* does not in itself guarantee its achievement. Things can go wrong: the tadpole may get eaten, the acorn may rot in the soil, and the man may be waylaid by his vices. Still, in general, nature is a self-sustaining harmonious order which affords each element within it the potential of its own distinctive self-completion. Such a view of nature contrasts strikingly with the modern view of physical nature as a causally governed, non-purposive system, and with modern man's consequently problematic relationship with this system. Where nature is not seen as possessing inherent purposiveness, human beings have to account for the normative significance of their existence in alternative terms. The compatibilist / incompatibilist debate, which has been a sub-theme of this book, represents two divergent ways in which to come to terms, morally, with the modern Newtonian world-view. In Aristotle, freedom is not thematized, and although Raz parts company with Aristotle in this respect, his normative naturalism allows him to sidestep the compatibilist / incomptabilist debate; indeed, it allows him to adopt an altogether more oblique approach to the meaning and normative significance of freedom than any of the writers examined thus far.

Of course, to attribute a normative naturalism to Raz is not to say that he shares Aristotle's general natural teleology – that he rejects the modern scientific understanding of the natural world. To suggest that Raz holds a version of Aristotelian normative naturalism is simply to suggest that he advocates a conception of normativity which is unusual when compared to standard liberal perspectives, in that it does not think of human beings as called upon to create their own order of value. Recall my depiction, in the last chapter, of Dworkin as a humanist. I suggested that Dworkin endorses an uncompromisingly humanistic view of man as the forger of his own destiny, as capable of realizing 'his own dreams', whatever they are. Interestingly, Raz himself makes a point of subscribing to a form of humanism: 'I will endorse right away the humanistic principle which claims that the explanation and justification of the goodness or badness of anything derives ultimately from its contribution, actual or possible, to human life and its quality.'[6] Yet Raz's humanist principle is much more modest than the position I attributed to Dworkin.[7] Although Raz does hold that the *justification* of values requires reference to how they impact upon individuals' lives, his claim is not that human beings are the *creators* of value.

In fact, Raz is intriguingly ambiguous about the source of values. The idea of a value is normative. For Raz, as for Aristotle, the idea of normativity is closely related in turn to human beings' capacity for reason.[8] Human reason is responsive to value, or, to put it somewhat differently, human reasoners 'perceive' value(s) in the world. Raz says that 'aspects of the world are normative, that is, they constitute reasons for action'.[9] Elsewhere he says, similarly, that 'rationality is the ability to respond appropriately to (perceived) normative aspects of the world'.[10] But what does Raz mean by 'normative aspects of the world'? More specifically, does he think that the existence of 'normative aspects of the world' is a function of the existence of reasoning human beings? In the absence of reasoning human beings, would there be *no* such normative aspects, or would human non-existence merely mean that these aspects would fail to be perceived as such by any reasoning beings? If, as seems likely, there would be no normative aspects in the absence of human existence, why not say that normative aspects attach to reasoning human beings rather than to the world? Indeed, why not say, as some of Raz's critics want to say, that reasoning human beings are the source of all normativity, hence of all value?[11]

Raz's reluctance to endorse the idea of human beings as the source or creators of values has much to do with his Aristotelian normative naturalism and his related suspicion of the voluntarism implicit in these stronger claims. Although the existence of normative aspects in the world must be 'traced back' to the existence of reasoning human beings, this does not mean that values are the product of human willing or choosing. The normative aspects of the world are as they are in virtue of the kind of beings that reasoning human beings are independently of their wills and choices. There are two normatively significant key features that stand out about the nature of reasoning human beings. The first is that such beings are physically embodied, needy beings. This feature of human beings explains the existence of what Raz defines as 'instrumental values', such as 'the value of the means of personal survival, such as food, shelter, good health'.[12] The second, and for our purposes more relevant normatively significant, feature concerns Raz's view of human beings as naturally reasoning social beings. Raz neither believes with Kant that reason is a non-natural normative capacity of human beings that somehow places them outside the natural order, nor thinks with Hume that reason is merely instrumentally valuable, that while necessary to the effective pursuit of what one wants, it is not itself the source of value. Instead, reason is a thoroughgoing normative yet nonetheless natural capacity of human persons. What is more, Raz is non-individualistic about human flourishing. He does not think that individual human beings could flourish outside society. Human beings naturally reason, and they naturally live in society with one another.

This second feature – or couplet of features – about human nature is of significance for what Raz calls 'intrinsic values' – values that have a non-instrumental purpose and that are valuable for their own sake. Friendship, love, justice and personal autonomy are reason-infused intrinsic values which can 'emerge' only in the social context where they are 'sustained' by social practices.[13] Again, it is not clear what precisely Raz means by the social 'emergence' of values. He insists that values emerge in the social context and that they are sustained by social practices even whilst resisting the thought that values are coextensive with social practices. His immediate concern is to avoid the charge of social relativism: Raz does not want to reduce values to social practices, making their validity relative to given social contexts. Values are sustained by social practices but non-reducible to them – indeed, he suggests that, once a value has 'emerged' within a given social context, it may persist even when relevant value-sustaining practices cease. This is perhaps an odd view, but one that is designed to underscore his denial that intrinsic values are reducible to social practices. Perhaps, when they cease to be practised, such values join the stock of socially forgotten values – such as the medieval value of chivalry – that now lie dormant but remain available for retrieval, at least in principle, at any time.[14]

Raz's fascinating if elusive position on values and their social emergence cannot detain us any longer. For present purposes I shall assume that when Raz speaks of the social emergence of non-relativistic intrinsic values, he has in mind values that arise non-voluntaristically from the normative status of human persons as naturally reasoning, naturally sociable human beings. Given the non-variability of normative human nature across societies, the intrinsic values that derive from its defining features have the capacity to transcend those social forms within the context of which they emerge initially. Of course, if Raz is correct about the value-sustaining role of social practices, the adoption of 'non-indigenous' values by other societies entails the further requirement upon such societies to adopt relevant value-sustaining social practices: and this is likely to result in broad-scale social change. Take the intrinsic value of personal autonomy, which according to Raz can properly emerge only within liberal forms of life. This does not mean that the value of personal autonomy has normative validity only within those contexts: to the contrary, in so far as it is an intrinsic value, personal autonomy can transcend the liberal context and can be adopted by non-liberal societies. Yet its adoption within non-liberal social contexts will have a more general impact on the type of social practices available in those societies, contributing to these societies' gradual transformation towards an ever more liberal form of social life. It is thus by means of his appeal to a version of neo-Aristotelian normative naturalism that Raz seeks to avoid both what he regards as the excessively abstract 'moral universalism' of more conventional liberal theorizing and the opposing danger of a slide into an excessively contextualized moral relativism.

III. Personal Autonomy as a Social Value

Reading *The Morality of Freedom*, it is noticeable how little direct reference to the idea of freedom it contains. Raz denies that we can gain an adequate understanding of any particular moral value or political principle by means of abstract philosophical analysis: 'neither a definition nor a conceptual analysis of "freedom" can solve our problems. What we need is not a definition nor mere conceptual clarity. What we require are moral principles and arguments to support them.'[15] Raz's rejection of 'mere conceptual clarity' is in keeping with his wider perfectionist commitments. One who believes that intrinsic values emerge from forms of social life is not going to find much use for conceptual analysis as a philosophical method that specifically abstracts from social context. For much of the time *MF* instead considers themes as seemingly wide-ranging as the justification of political authority, the nature and limits of rights, the idea of personal well-being, the incommensurability of values. This can be disconcerting for one looking for a more direct approach to freedom. Yet, given Raz's general philosophical outlook, he can nonetheless justifiably claim that 'the whole purpose of the book is to defend a concept of political freedom'.[16] The perfectionist concept of political freedom emerges from an examination and understanding of sustaining political institutions and social practices and cannot be analysed apart from these.

As it is, Raz does not turn directly to the idea of freedom until the final two chapters of the book. Even then, he says little about the negative / positive distinction. He accepts the distinction, but does not see the two concepts as mutually exclusive interpretations of freedom.[17] There is a place for negative freedom within liberal societies, but there is equally a place for positive freedom. By and large, the two complement one another. Negative freedom is 'freedom from coercive interferences',[18] especially interferences by the law. Positive freedom is 'the capacity for autonomy'.[19] (I shall say more about this below.) What binds negative and positive freedom together is the value of personal autonomy: 'negative freedom is valuable inasmuch as it serves positive freedom and autonomy'. Similarly, 'one's positive freedom is enhanced by whatever enhances one's ability to lead an autonomous life'.[20] The overall value of freedom is the value of personal autonomy. Since Raz is interested primarily in the *value* of freedom, his discussion from then on focuses squarely on the idea of personal autonomy.

We saw that, on the perfectionist view, governments do and ought to promote values and value-sustaining social practices. The value of personal autonomy, Raz says, is 'a fact of life'[21] in contemporary liberal societies: 'in western industrial societies a particular conception of individual well-being has acquired considerable popularity. It is the idea of personal autonomy.'[22] By this, Raz does not mean that more and more people have chosen to embrace the ideal of personal autonomy because, in Dworkin's terms, they find it to be an 'attractive ideal'. For perfectionists the adoption of a value is not a matter of choice. When a given value, such as the value of personal autonomy, emerges within a given form of social life, people get exposed to it through its sustaining social practices. They come to perceive the practice as valuable, and conduct their lives in conformity with it. But this does not mean that they *decide* to endorse the value of autonomy, or that they *choose* to become autonomous. In many ways, Raz claims, people living in liberal societies have little choice *but* to be autonomous. Social and political life is arranged around this value, and it will as a matter of fact be difficult for individual persons to exempt themselves from its socially pervasive influence upon them. If this sounds sinister to some, then all that can be said at the moment is that it is not meant to be: Raz is not saying that any social practice that happens to emerge counts as valuable merely in virtue of the fact that it has so emerged. He is not a social relativist. One can tell the difference between valuable and non-valuable social practices by noting how well or how badly they correspond with normative naturalism – by how well or how badly they contribute to human flourishing.

I shall return to the non-voluntary nature of valuing personal autonomy below. For now it suffices to point out that, if one accepts Raz's general Aristotelian picture of the social emergence of values, the thought is far more intuitive than it otherwise might be that governments have a role in promoting and sustaining social values. In many ways, governments simply *are* best placed to promote and regulate social practices that help sustain the value of personal autonomy. They can do so by means of negative and positive freedom measures. The promotion of autonomy by negative means might take the form of removing legal constraints on certain actions; its positive promotion might either be general and indirect, as the design and implementation of a specifically *liberal* curriculum in state schools which exposes children to liberal values in general; or it can be specifically targeted, such as when contraceptives are made freely available through the national health system in order to encourage women to gain control over their reproductive role. Importantly, negative and positive freedom measures are equally substantive forms of autonomy promotion. Negative measures have nothing to do with government standing back and withholding moral judgement: negative freedom measures are intended to 'serve' positive freedom and autonomy. By the same token, negative promotional actions are not in themselves sufficient: 'there is more one can do to help another person have an autonomous life than stand off and refrain from coercing and manipulating him'.[23]

Unsurprisingly, Raz's contention that liberal governments can and do institute autonomy-promoting laws and social policies – indeed, that they ought to do so – has met with resistance from among those liberals – most – who do not share his underlying Aristotelianism. Liberal neutralists of libertarian and of egalitarian persuasions alike are united in their complaint that, in prescribing to individuals what is good for them, perfectionism treats them like children, thereby acting paternalistically towards them, *denying* them, in effect, their autonomy. Conversely, if Raz is content to shoulder the burden of this charge, endorsing 'paternalistic measures which encourage the adoption of valuable ends and discourage the pursuit of bad ones',[24] this is precisely because he does not share his critics' view of autonomy as an individual value or attribute – as an object of individual choice or possession over which each individual has sovereign control. Even so, Raz does acknowledge the special nature of the value of autonomy and the constraints imposed upon its promotion by governments:

> Since autonomy is morally valuable there is reason for everyone to make himself and everyone else autonomous. But it is the special character of autonomy that one cannot make another person autonomous. One can bring the horse to the water but one cannot make it drink. One is autonomous if one determines the course of one's life by oneself. This is not to say that others cannot help, but their help is by and large confined to securing the background conditions which enable a person to be autonomous.[25]

Governments cannot coercively enforce autonomy, but can at best enhance persons' capacity for autonomy. So what, more precisely, is the (social) value of autonomy? What is it to be autonomous, and what does the capacity for autonomy comprise?

III. 1. The value of personal autonomy

What is it to be autonomous? Superficially, Raz circumscribes what he calls personal autonomy in standard liberal terms, drawing a close association between autonomy and choice. He explicitly distances his account of personal autonomy from Kantian conceptions of moral autonomy: 'personal autonomy, which is a particular ideal of individual well-being, should not be confused with the only very indirectly related [Kantian] idea of moral autonomy. Kantian moral autonomy is a doctrine about the nature of morality. Personal autonomy is no more than one specific moral idea which, if valid, is one element in a moral doctrine.'[26] Kantian moral autonomy is concerned with the idea of moral self-legislation: individuals subject their power of choice to the demands of the categorical imperative as supreme principle or law of morality. When it is not simply conflated with Millian autonomy, Kant's position is frequently read as advocating a form of moral asceticism or self-denial. Raz seems to share this view.[27] As with Dworkin, so Raz's delimitation of the meaning of personal autonomy is more consonant with the Millian ideal of personal independence: 'The ruling idea behind the ideal of personal autonomy is that people should make their own lives. The autonomous person is a (part) author of his own life. The ideal of personal autonomy is the vision of people controlling, to some degree, their own destiny, fashioning it through successive decisions throughout their lives.'[28] Again, 'autonomy is opposed to a life of coerced choices. It contrasts with a life of no choices, or of drifting through life without ever exercising one's capacity for choice.'[29] The ideal of autonomy is the ideal of 'a life freely chosen';[30] 'the life of the autonomous person consists of pursuits freely chosen from various alternatives which were open to him';[31] indeed, the ideal is connected with the 'creation of new values and reasons'.[32]

The moral importance of choice suffuses Raz's comments no less than it does mainstream, non-perfectionist autonomy accounts.[33] At first blush, this is surprising – disappointing even. Given Raz's wary attitude towards the moral individualism of mainstream liberalism, one might have expected less emphasis on the idea of the autonomous person as a 'chooser' of their own life. However, initial impressions may mislead here: after all, Raz specifically rejects the view of autonomy itself as a possible object of individual choice, arguing that persons come to value autonomy in consequence of their social exposure to it. And indeed, even within the context of autonomy itself, Raz regards the value of choice as dependent on the value of personal autonomy. While choice is important in so far as its exercise is conducive to autonomy, it is not intrinsically valuable. This view explains Raz's rejection of a number of familiar specifications of the value of autonomy that emphasize the independent value of choice. He denies, for example, that the value of autonomy amounts to the value of self-realization: 'Self-realization consists in the development to their full extent of all, or all the valuable capacities a person possesses. The autonomous person is the one who makes his own life and he may choose the path of self-realization or not.'[34] The ideal of self-realization has connotations of a person's possessing complete voluntary control over their actions and development of their capacities: that they choose to make themselves into who they are.[35] It is arguably an overly ambitious ideal under virtually any description, and thus unsurprisingly rejected by Raz. Yet Raz also repudiates the more modest ideal of the autonomous life as a unified life. The ideal of giving one's life unity is implicit in Dworkin's challenge conception, which compares a successful life to a brilliant dive into the pool the elegance and accomplishment of which linger with the spectator even after the ripples have died down. Contained within this image of the accomplished diver is an admonishment towards giving our lives a determinate overall shape. Raz rejects this ideal, too: 'The ideal of personal autonomy is not to be identified with the ideal of giving one's life a unity. An autonomous person's well-being consists in the successful pursuit of self-chosen goals and relationships. It does not require an attempt to impose unity on one's life.'[36]

Instead, a pleasingly modest conception of the autonomous life emerges from Raz's account. The ideal of autonomy is not articulated with reference to extraordinary powers of choice and control voluntaristically conceived. At one level, autonomy is simply the way of life thrust upon persons living in liberal societies. Liberal society expects us to be autonomous, and we expect the same of ourselves in a variety of ways which it mostly does not occur to us to describe in autonomy-invoking terms. Liberal society expects us to take major decisions regarding the course of our lives: work, marriage partner, children, religious denomination – decisions that will shape our lives, setting us on paths which we might not have ended up on had we chosen differently. Take marriage as an example. The idea of marriage as a voluntary union between two people who have selected one another for a life together is such a commonplace in contemporary liberal societies that most would not associate it with the ideal of autonomy.[37] Yet this particular type of marital practice may look rather odd to persons who have grown up in non-liberal contexts. Marriage by choice belongs to those many autonomy-promoting liberal social practices and legal institutions from which it is in fact difficult to escape in liberal societies. Similarly with the idea of career choice: we routinely ask young children what they want to be when they grow up. Children routinely respond by offering a ranked list of preferred career choices. Most will not end up doing what they think they want to do – most will follow versions of their parents' type of employment: but this fact does little to undermine our theoretical confidence in the desirability of choice with regard to career decisions. Even in the area of child bearing and parenting, Raz points out, technological developments have given persons living in liberal societies a much greater degree of control over when and how to have children.

Although choices of this kind have a decisive influence on the overall direction of an ordinary person's life, they are rarely explicitly associated with 'more intellectualized'[38] versions of the ideal of personal autonomy. It is an advantage of Raz's approach that he casts personal autonomy as a way of life that is in principle achievable, albeit to varying degrees, by most of those living in liberal societies. Razian personal autonomy does require a certain kind of commitment: it demands that persons be loyal to their choices, and that they do not abandon their chosen paths at a whim: 'the commitment to a particular course of action creates new reasons which one did not have before'.[39] One who has previously chosen marital life and has started a family should not simply up sticks and leave when a tempting job offer comes along on the other side of the world. Personal autonomy requires the ability to *forgo* attractive choices in the light of commitments already entered into:

> having embraced certain goals and commitments we create new ways of succeeding and new ways of failing. In embracing goals and commitments, in coming to care about one thing or

another, one progressively gives shape to one's life, determines what would count as a successful life and what would be a failure. One creates values, generates through one's developing commitments and pursuits reasons which transcend the reasons one had for undertaking one's commitments and pursuits.[40]

Again, the emphasis is less on choice itself than on a preparedness to live with one's choices, including taking on unanticipated commitments that come with marital life, parenting, career choices. One must be prepared *not* to exert voluntaristic control over one's life but to let oneself be directed instead by new normative reasons and commitments that arise from one's previous choices.[41] There are, of course, problems with Raz's modest account of what it is to be autonomous. For one thing, it may feel just a little too homely – the focus on domestic examples, though realistic, does not help here. But relegating the independent moral significance of choice may itself seem worrying, especially once it emerges that, for Raz, the overall value of autonomy lies in the value of pursuing *good* options (more on this below). If to be valuable, choices have to be good choices, why do these good things need to be chosen at all? What, on Raz's account, does the fact that it was chosen add to the value of pursuing a valuable option? Indeed, what does autonomy add to the value of pursuing the good life? If a life is only as good as the activities it is comprised of, why insist on the *autonomous* pursuit of these activities? Raz's modest account of personal autonomy may be so choice depreciating as to make it difficult to recognize it as a version of liberal autonomy at all. We shall return to these issues in section IV, but must first consider what Raz means by the 'capacity for autonomy'.

III. 2. The capacity for autonomy

Raz defines positive freedom as referring to the 'capacity for autonomy'. This is in keeping with the positive tradition so long as one takes those capacities to refer to aspects of a person's internal constitution – to their mental capacities, say, or their psychological attitudes. Unusually, Raz's capacity account departs from such an exclusive focus on agent-internal requirements: 'much of the writing on autonomy focuses on an agent's ability to form informed and effective judgements as a condition for autonomy. There can be no doubt of its importance. But there are additional aspects to autonomy as (part) authorship of one's life. One is relational: an autonomous person is not subject to the will of another. Another aspect of autonomy concerns the quality of the options open to agents.'[42] Razian capacity for autonomy thus comprises three components: (a) the agent-internal possession of certain mental capacities; (b) the agent-external availability of an adequate range of options; and (c) the relational requirement of independence. Raz says least about (c) and most about (b). I shall here follow his example, focusing primarily on requirement (b) – 'an adequate range of options'.

Briefly, the requirement of independence refers to the demand for non-coercion and non-manipulation: 'all coercion invades autonomy by subjecting the will of the coerced'. Hence it is a condition of autonomy not only that agents respect one another's capacity to judge and decide for themselves, but also that governments do so: while governments may promote certain autonomy-enhancing options, they may not force persons to take up and pursue these options.[43] With regard to (a) – possession of mental capacities – Raz's overall account is Aristotelian. By way of contrast, recall Nozick's decisionistic approach to practical rationality. On Nozick's account, agents decide in the act of weighing and weighting different possible options which one is the best, in the sense of most preferred, option for them. On this model, when a rationally competent person *decides* that option X is of no value to them, then that option really is of no value to them. Raz, on the other hand, thinks of human reasoners as responsive to normative aspects of the world. Reasoning agents *perceive* value in the world – they do not *decide* whether a given option is or is not of value. In relation to their capacity for autonomy, a person's choices should ideally enhance their well-being. Well-being is a form of Aristotelian eudaimonia for Raz: apart from the satisfaction of instrumentally valuable things – health, nourishment, shelter, etc. – it includes the pursuit of intrinsically valuable projects and goals, such as friendships, satisfying work, loving family relations, and so on. Practically reasoning persons are responsive to these normative well-being requirements, which they have in virtue of the kind of beings they are. For Raz, successful practical reasoning consists in making the right kind of judgements with regard to the well-being options that are objectively available to a person. Making the 'right kind of judgements' consists in the adoption and pursuit of those good options that are most appropriate to a person's temperament and circumstances. Practical deliberation is not about deciding which options are valuable and which not: it is about judging aright which valuable option to pursue under which circumstances.

The link between Raz's Aristotelian account of practical deliberation and (b) – an adequate range of options – is a strong one. In so far as the value of autonomy lies in the pursuit of a particular form of the good life, in so far as the goodness of a life is a function of the goodness of the options pursued, and in so far as persons' capacity for practical reason consists in responsiveness to the goodness of options available to them, persons' opportunity adequately to exercise their reasoning capacities largely depends on the availability of an adequate range of good options. It is the social context directly, and government indirectly, that makes these good options available. Here, two closely related themes emerge that require more extended consideration. The first is the idea of value pluralism and related value incommensurability. The second is the – contentious – requirement upon liberal government to make available only morally good options.

Liberal governments have a duty, Raz says, to provide an adequate range of options as a condition of persons' capacity for autonomy. Governments may not coerce persons to be autonomous – nonetheless, they should encourage persons to exercise their capacity for autonomy. We saw above that governments can adopt a variety of negative and positive freedom measures towards this end: the lifting of legal restrictions or the provision of certain types of education or health care facilities represent negative and positive such measures respectively. It is important to remember that, on Raz's account, a government's decision to pass this or that law, or to adopt this or that social policy, ought to reflect a concern with personal autonomy as a substantive social value. Governments revoke the illegality of same-sex marriage not on non-interference grounds but on the grounds that so doing will enhance the capacity for autonomy of a particular subsection of the population. Again, governments make available free contraception not so as to expand the scope of mere sheer sexual choice, but on the grounds that such availability will enhance a given group's capacity for autonomy with regard to their reproductive role.

It is, however, a peculiar feature of the value of personal autonomy that, in exercising their capacity for it, different persons will be responsive to different values and options available to them. It is not the case that 'one size fits all'. While the removal of legal constraints upon same-sex marriage will enhance the capacity for autonomy of some, it will make no difference to others' autonomy capacities. Similarly, with the provision of free contraceptives. More generally, public funding of the arts, provision of sports facilities, protection of places of worship, etc. will always be of importance to the personal well-being opportunities of some but not others. The value of personal autonomy thus carries value pluralism in its train. Different persons will choose to pursue different values. Raz acknowledges that within liberal societies a plurality of good ways of life should be deemed equally permissible such that their pursuit should be made equally possible: '[different] forms of life are not only morally legitimate but also ones which need to be available if all persons are to have autonomy'.[44] Again, 'autonomy requires that many morally acceptable options be available to a person'.[45] Governments must provide an adequate *range* of options – a range from which different persons will be able to choose different options even though none of them will be able to choose all options.

It is in this connection that Raz's discussion of value *incommensurability* emerges as an interesting liberal variation on Aristotelian virtue ethics. According to Aristotle, the *eudaimon* will respond appropriately to each practical situation as it arises, and in so doing will exercise different virtues of the broad palette of virtues available. In a sense, the *eudaimon* has mastered all the virtues and applies them appropriately on each occasion. According to Raz, by contrast, the pursuit of some virtues (or values) will in itself preclude the possible pursuit of others: the pursuit of some values is incommensurate with that of others.[46] By the same token, individual members of liberal society must be tolerant of one another's divergent conceptions of the good life. Indeed, value incommensurability has the consequence not only that we cannot each embrace the pursuit of all values: it has the further interesting consequence that some of the wider normative commitments which we endorse as a result of pursuing a particular form of the good life will result in a tendency to be impatient with regard to the normative commitments entered into by others.[47] Take a banal example: a person who is devoted to the pursuit of a career which they find personally fulfilling will often be impatient with the attitudes and commitments of one who has devoted themselves to being a good parent. While the careerist will be able to perceive value in being a good parent, they will nonetheless find themselves driven to distraction by the parent's patient engagement with an endless list of seemingly pointless questions posed by the parent's children. Similarly, while the parent is able to discern value in the careerist's single-minded pursuit of their work, they will often be frustrated by the other's lack of attention to other aspects of human life.

Controversially, although Raz demands that government and individual members of liberal society be tolerant even of persons' morally bad choices and practices – at least within the constraints of the law[48] – he nonetheless denies that governments have a duty to include bad options among the promotion of an 'adequate range of options'. In itself, non-promotion of bad options is hardly contentious: the controversy centres on Raz's insistence that governments have a duty to make available morally good options. That governments should not promote morally bad options seems obvious: they can at best be required to tolerate them as an unavoidable fact of life. Given human nature, people will make bad choices, some more so than others. Importantly, Raz sees nothing valuable at all in the making of bad choices. The making of bad choices now is not a spur to the making of better choices in the future, for example. Contrast this with Dworkin's responsibility principle, whose requirement that persons bear the costs of their bad choices could be read as including an educational dimension. On such a reading there is something good about making bad choices: the (potential) goodness of bad choices lies in the opportunity for improvement which their commission affords. Raz explicitly rejects such a view: while 'opportunities for the immoral and repugnant cannot be eliminated from our world',[49] it does not follow that 'the availability of such options is a requirement of respect for autonomy'.[50] The one does not entail the other, among other things because evil is not the whetstone of virtue: whatever sound sense there is in this view derives, according to Raz, from the thought that the morally good would have been good even in the face of opportunities for evil.

Raz's view that bad choices have no reformative or educational element in relation to future choices tallies with his view that autonomy requires the availability only of good choices, and that autonomy-respecting governments ought to promote only good options. Advocates of liberal neutrality object to this stance because of the spectre of paternalism raised by it. Neutralists deny that governments have a duty to promote either bad options or good ones: they hold that each individual ought to be left to discover for themselves what the good life consist in for them. In committing themselves to this position, neutralists do seem to endorse a view of individual choice – good or bad – as intrinsically valuable. For Raz, by contrast, choice is valuable only in so far as it is in the service of autonomy. But autonomy, in turn, 'is valuable only if exercised in pursuit of the good. The ideal of autonomy requires only the availability of morally acceptable options.'[51] Hence, although an autonomy-respecting government has a duty to ensure the availability of an adequate range of options, given that the value of autonomy is a function of the goodness of the options pursued, there is no governmental duty to ensure the availability of non-valuable, non-autonomy-enhancing bad options.

IV. Perfectionist Autonomy Evaluated: Reason, Choice and Circumstance

We have seen that, according to Raz's neo-Aristotelian approach, personal autonomy is not an ideal which persons living in liberal societies can plausibly be said to choose to embrace. The social value of personal autonomy emerges within the liberal form of life and is sustained by liberal social practices and institutions. Persons are exposed to this ideal and come to value it in consequence of such non-voluntary exposure to it. Personal autonomy is nonetheless not a socially relative value. It is objectively valuable in so far as it is consonant with human flourishing and personal well-being. As such, it is capable of transcending liberal borders. Still, personal autonomy can be sustained only through appropriate liberal social practices. The promotion of these practices is the role of government. Liberal governments create the general social conditions under which persons' exercise of their capacity for personal autonomy becomes feasible. In so doing, they simultaneously create an environment that makes evasion of that ideal difficult:

> The value of personal autonomy is a fact of life. Since we live in a society whose social forms are to a considerable extent based on individual choice, and since our options are limited by what is available in our society, we can prosper in it only if we can be successfully autonomous. We may do so to varying degrees. Some people may base more of their lives on those aspects, such as parenthood, where choice is more limited. Others may improvise in their own lives and vary common forms to minimize the degree of choice in them. But ultimately those who live in an autonomy-enhancing culture can prosper only by being autonomous.[52]

The thought that persons living in liberal societies have the value of personal autonomy socially thrust upon them is an unusual one. Mainstream liberal approaches usually argue the other way round. Take Dworkin, according to whom liberal institutions ought to be based on values embraced independently by liberal citizens. Dworkin believes 'ethical individualism' to be a widely endorsed ideal in liberal societies, such that liberal social and legal liberal institutions should be shaped according to that ideal. Dworkin's is a more familiar, more intuitive, liberal starting point: we ascribe freedom or autonomy to ourselves and then design social institutions in accordance with such self-ascription. Yet, although more familiar intuitively, there is much, phenomenologically, to recommend Raz's position. Raz rightly points out that liberal institutions and social practices are in fact structured in ways that exert considerable pressure on persons to act autonomously. Contemporary liberal societies are both multicultural and value-pluralistic. The former feature in particular often invites the impression that, under liberalism, the pursuit of non-liberal individual conceptions of the good life is just as possible as that of liberal such conceptions. Raz rightly contests this assumption: it is very difficult for non-autonomy-valuing cultural communities fully to participate in the liberal social and political way of life without in so doing compromising their non-liberal practices: 'an autonomy-supporting culture offers its members opportunities which cannot be had in a non-autonomous environment, and lacks most of those opportunities available in the latter'.[53] It is objectively more difficult to pursue a more community-oriented way of life within the strictures of liberal social, legal and political arrangements – a way of life, for example, in which arranged marriages and a gender-based division of labour form important social practices sustaining the value of communal living. Liberal societies may tolerate such practices within immigrant communities, but the price to be paid by the latter is their effective exclusion from full social and political participation in the liberal social form of life.

A second important contribution of Raz's approach lies in the 'non-intellectualized' account it offers of the value of personal autonomy. Raz's focus is on the seemingly mundane, yet life-forming, areas of decision-making competence which the liberal individual is charged with – decisions involving marital life, career choices, parenting and so on. I commended Raz's pleasingly modest account of personal autonomy, contrasting it with Dworkin's challenge model, which remains wedded to unrealistically high expectations of personal excellence. There is nonetheless a puzzle about Razian liberal autonomy: it concerns the role of individual choice in relation to personal autonomy as a social value. While Raz's relegation of the independent value of choice is commendable for the reasons just summarized,[54] it nonetheless raises awkward questions about the independent value of personal autonomy. Raz begins by emphasizing the non-voluntary because social nature of valuing personal autonomy. Later he suggests that the value of individual choice depends on the value of personal autonomy. Clearly, on this view, choice and autonomy are not synonymous. Yet, later still Raz also argues that the value of autonomy is a function of the goodness of the options pursued: 'autonomy is valuable only if exercised in pursuit of the good'. It looks as though the value of choice depends on the value of personal autonomy, and the value of personal autonomy depends upon the value of the options pursued. But if the value both of choice and of personal autonomy depends upon the value of options pursued, why bother about either choice or personal autonomy? Why not go straight to the pursuit of good options?

I fear that my objection is difficult to state with lucidity. But consider the following imaginary scenario: person P is confronted with socially available mutually exclusive options A, B and C. Each of these options is of roughly equal value, such that opting for any of them will equally ensure P's flourishing. Given this, does it matter which of these options P chooses? Does it matter whether P chooses A over B or C? If I understand Raz correctly, then the act of choosing A does not in itself add anything to the value of A: the value of A is independent of the act of choosing A. In that sense, it would appear to be a matter of indifference whether P chooses A, B or C, given that all of them are of equal value, and given that the act of choice adds no value in itself. But if it is indifferent, in that sense, which of these options P chooses, is it not also indifferent whether or not P chooses any of them? Why not just assign to P option A? Since A, B and C are all equally valuable in the sense of contributing equally to P's flourishing, it really seems not to matter whether or not P chooses A or is assigned A.

It is difficult to suppress the impression that, from an autonomy perspective, it does matter whether P chooses A or is assigned A: it is difficult to avoid the thought that the act of choice itself adds value to the chosen option. On the one hand, Raz seems to think so too: he seems to think that the opportunity to decide for themselves enhances persons' well-being objectively conceived. Raz seems to want to say that making the right kind of choices – good choices – is valuable. But he does not want to concede that choosing is valuable in itself, or intrinsically so. If he were to concede this, he would also have to concede that there is something valuable even about bad choices. Yet to someone with Raz's perfectionist persuasions this would be like saying that something that is bad is (also) something that is good, or at any rate, that there is some good aspect to this bad option: namely, the fact that it was chosen. But if, to avoid saying those things, Raz says that the value of good choices lies in their goodness, whilst the disvalue of bad choices lies in their badness, it looks as though the notion of choice is doing no work at all: Raz could equally well say that the value of goodness is its goodness and the disvalue of badness its badness.

The worry is that the value of choice and, possibly, of autonomy, is an idle wheel in Raz's overall account of personal well-being and flourishing. Put differently, the worry is that the Aristotelian account of human flourishing and the liberal value of personal autonomy ultimately fail to engage with one another. The idea of choice plays no role, so far as I know, in Aristotle's ethics. According to Aristotle, persons are socially induced into practising the virtues. A person is habituated into the virtues until these become second nature, and the person learns to appraise aright each practical situation and to respond to it appropriately by 'mobilizing' the relevant virtue. Choice does not come into it, though practical judgement does. Raz is clearly taken by the Aristotelian account of practical deliberation – by the idea that we perceive and respond appropriately to normative aspects of the world. In this distinctive, non-modern conception of natural practical deliberation, Raz discovers a powerful antidote to modern voluntaristic accounts of practical rationality and choice. He seems intent upon retrieving an ideal of liberal autonomy that is not tied to voluntaristic choice: his difficulty is that Aristotelian practical reasoning is so far removed from the idea of choice as to make it a moral irrelevance in Raz's perfectionist account of human flourishing. It seems difficult to subscribe to a version of Aristotelian normative naturalism according to which, given human nature, some things are either good or bad for persons, and simultaneously to endorse the idea that the good life is a function, centrally, of a person's choices about what they take to be good for them.

Given this difficulty, what seems odd is not so much the fact that Raz does not simply abandon the ideal of personal autonomy and confine himself to a more stringent form of Aristotelian virtue ethics instead: what seems odd is his failure to attempt a more systematic severance of the mainstream liberal tie between autonomy and choice.[55] Instead of conceding more scope than he seems comfortable doing to the centrality of choice, why not assign pride of place to the notion of judgement instead? After all, while the notion of choice plays no role in Aristotelian virtue ethics at all, practical judgement is central to it: so instead of saying that being autonomous is to make good choices, why not say that autonomy is a function of good practical judgement? In many ways an emphasis on judgement over choice tallies better with Raz's requirement of a preparedness to give oneself over to the wider normative reasons and commitments entailed by one's initial 'choices': to be autonomous is to judge certain courses of possible action inappropriate for one, given the commitments one has already entered into. Choice is a misnomer here. This is a point well made more generally by Claudia Mills: we do not in practice make half as many choices with regard to important aspects of our lives as the liberal literature on the subject tends to have us believe – although we do make practical judgements. Most of us do not really choose our spouses from a range of alternative options available to us: we judge this or that person who happened to come along suitable for the purpose.[56] Most of us do not choose between either following a career in academic research or becoming a sky-diving instructor: in general, the thought is ludicrous that the aspiring academic would have been just as suited to becoming a sky-diver. We find ourselves drawn to particular types of activity and, if we are very lucky, end up at a certain point earning a living from them. Nor do most of us choose to have children: we mostly simply have them and (luckily for them and for ourselves) judge having had them to be a good thing on balance.

To a large extent, Raz's pleasingly modest account of the value of personal autonomy is deflationary with regard to the mainstream liberal emphasis on the independent value of choice; but this makes it difficult to understand why, in the end, Raz retains the connection between autonomy and choice. That he does so is all the more puzzling in view of the prominent role assigned by Aristotle to the idea of practical judgement. An emphasis on judgement over choice might have brought out the deep connection that Raz clearly perceives between our status as reasoning beings who see value in the world and the value of personal autonomy as lying in making the right kind of judgements with regard to those aspects of our lives that are most important for our flourishing and personal well-being. On the diagnosis offered here, to the extent to which Raz's perfectionist account of liberal autonomy does ultimately fail to persuade, this is not because of his downgrading of the independent value of choice, but because of his apparent reluctance, despite such downgrading, to sever more decisively the perceived tie between liberal autonomy and voluntaristic choice.

Conclusion: Liberal Freedom – Negative, Positive, Either or Neither?

This book has offered a partial survey and assessment of ongoing freedom debates within contemporary liberal political philosophy. Starting with Berlin's seminal distinction between the negative and positive concepts of liberal freedom, one of the aims here has been to ask why, despite repeated challenges to that distinction, it resiliently returns to structure disagreement about the meaning and normative significance of liberal freedom. This resilience is all the more surprising in view of the fact that it is often genuinely difficult to assign particular thinkers unambiguously to either camp: Berlin found this difficult with regard to Mill; the current book has encountered the same problem in the case of Dworkin. Even when thinkers such as Nozick and Steiner clearly state and adhere to their commitment to negative freedom, their respective accounts of the grounds and ends of negative freedom differ from one another, with Nozick building on a highly individualistic metaphysics of free will in contrast to Steiner's more Kantian, relational presuppositions. Similarly with the two approaches to positive freedom examined in this book. Although both Dworkin's and Raz's work betray a debt to the autonomy conception contained in the writings of Mill, each absorbs these differently into their broader philosophical outlook and method of approach. Dworkin's humanism reflects the positivistic strands within Mill's position; Raz draws on its teleological aspects, combining these with an

Aristotelian normative naturalism. The resulting autonomy conceptions place contrasting emphases on individual independence and socially mediated human flourishing, respectively. Again, there are cross-cutting allegiances: Nozick and Dworkin are both more individualistic in their conceptions of freedom, while Steiner and Raz are more relational. Nonetheless, deep methodological and metaphysical divisions remain: Nozick is an incompatibilist about free will, whilst Dworkin draws from compatibilist resources; Steiner is committed to a highly abstract normative formalism, whereas Raz endorses a substantive normative naturalism.

These cross-cutting overlaps and divisions may invite the conclusion that there are, perhaps, not one or even just two liberal conceptions of freedom, but innumerably many possible interpretations of this strikingly elusive concept. Recall my mention in chapter 2 of what used to be a fairly widespread characterization of freedom as an 'essentially contested concept' – one with regard to the meaning and significance of which perennial dispute and disagreement are to be expected. Although there is some truth in this characterization, the notion of a concept as essentially *contested* has unfortunate political connotations, invoking the image of a 'battlefield' of ideas, with contestants driven by conflicting ideological designs and ambitions. This picture portrays things back to front. Political differences do exist between a libertarian such as Nozick and a perfectionist such as Raz. But more often than not, political differences are a *consequence* of freedom disagreements, not their source. It is not so much that we differ in our conceptions of freedom because we have conflicting political commitments; rather, we have conflicting political commitments because we differ in our conceptions of freedom.

It has been a major concern of this book to set out and engage with the specific methodological and metaphysical presuppositions of different liberal writers' theories of freedom. In part, this concern grew out of a more general dissatisfaction with the still widespread trend in current liberal theorizing to 'remain on the surface philosophically' – to set aside issues of metaphysical disagreement in order to focus on the possibility of reaching political agreement. In relation to the concept of freedom, the assumption remains common that when it comes to discussing the politics of freedom, the metaphysics of free will can safely be set aside, since disagreements at that level have no bearing on how we might arrange ourselves politically. This view operates with a strangely disengaged conception of the role of metaphysics in philosophical and ordinary thinking. Our metaphysical presuppositions reflect our most basic beliefs about the nature and structure of the (human) universe. While for that reason admittedly hardest to justify, they are also the basic road-markings that guide each of our respective inquiries. It is a fact of philosophical life that the same world genuinely makes sense to the compatibilist in a way that is very different from how the incompatibilist is constrained to comprehend it. These differences do have normative consequences. This is why it is often difficult to shed the suspicion that those who demand a setting aside of metaphysical beliefs and presuppositions unwittingly cling to theirs, describing as mere common sense what may nonetheless not appear as such to those who do not share those deepest underlying, if unacknowledged, commitments.

Often the refusal to engage with a thinker's explicit or implicit metaphysics issues in (unintended) distortion of their normative theory. We saw this with regard to Nozick's libertarianism: is it really so counterintuitive to say that the thief is not free to enter a house which he is nonetheless able to enter? I suggested that whether or not one thinks this depends largely on one's metaphysics of freedom. If Nozick does not find his position counterintuitive, this is because he expects persons to whom it is possible to ascribe freedom to be cognizant of others' legitimate freedom claims. This may be an expectation which those of a more descriptive philosophical bent don't share: but that does not in itself render Nozick's view implausible. A different example is the attribution to Dworkin of a supposedly unattractive incompatibilist conception of choice on the grounds of his unforgiving responsibility principle. This *is* implausible: Dworkin's emphasis on character building and his admonishment that we should learn from our mistakes makes him a much more likely sympathizer with compatibilist accounts of responsibility attribution.

Examining a thinker's underlying metaphysics not only helps guard against possible misattribution and other confusions: it can also enable a deeper understanding of the distinctiveness of their normative position. Take Raz's emphasis on personal autonomy as a *social* value: it is difficult to understand this as much more than a somewhat contrary rejection of mainstream liberal individualism unless one appreciates the subtlety and sophistication of the more general normative naturalism which informs Raz's autonomy account. Similarly, the elegance of Steiner's sparsely descriptive approach may elude one in the absence of unearthing the unusual admixture of Hobbesian and Kantian freedom presuppositions which informs it.

One might retort, of course, that allowing oneself to be guided by different writers' divergent freedom commitments at the metaphysical level exacts a high price normatively. I conceded just now that, instead of reducing Berlin's two concepts of liberty to one cogent overall liberal freedom account, the approach taken here appears to have yielded a proliferation of by and large equally plausible conceptions of liberal freedom. Should this not be worrying? Perhaps the disappointed reader will protest that they came to this book seeking guidance about the meaning of liberal freedom, but are left with a subset of different equally possible approaches none of which leaves them any the wiser regarding the *truth* about liberal freedom. But there may *be* no truth about liberal freedom.

By contrast with, say, the concept of a chair, the concept of freedom is elusive. It is not a determinate concept, the necessary and sufficient constitutive components of which are reasonably straightforward to identify and relate to one another. In a sense, the elusiveness of the concept of freedom is most appreciated by Steiner, who, before setting out on his descriptive route, acknowledges the immense diversity in ordinary language usages and meanings of 'freedom' – a diversity which Steiner admits no freedom theory is capable of capturing fully, such that the theorist is constrained to cull conflicting freedom intuitions. Clearly, such culling entails that no single theory of freedom is capable of offering an exhaustive analysis and account of its 'real' meaning. The *concept* of freedom is indeterminate: this is why, strictly speaking, talk of the *idea* of freedom seems to me preferable. To speak of freedom as an idea is to resist the otherwise unavoidable pressure towards complete conceptual specification. It is to acknowledge that the meaning of freedom is in many ways indeterminate, or open-ended.

This is not to say that there are no recurring themes in the accounts of freedom of the liberal thinkers here examined. There is considerable overlap concerning certain basic features. Most obvious is the notion of a necessary connection between a person's freedom and others' non-interference with that person. For some thinkers, physical non-interference is a sufficient freedom condition; others believe mental non-interference to be at least as important. Of the thinkers here examined, only Raz is a little circumspect about the unconditional status of non-interference as a freedom requirement. Raz holds negative freedom to be valuable only in so far as it is conducive to positive freedom. This is a strong statement; it may be taken to imply that interference which is conducive to positive freedom is likewise valuable. In fact, this is unlikely: Raz also holds that no one can be forced to be free – his view is not that *if* autonomy could be had by other means, non-interference would not be a requirement for it; rather, it is that in the absence of non-interference, autonomy would not be possible. At the other extreme of the non-interference requirement is Steiner's contention that physical non-prevention is a necessary and sufficient condition of freedom. On Steiner's account, another's coercive threats do not render a person unfree. This, too, is a strong claim to make. It severely restricts the descriptive account's scope for negative (un)freedom attributions. Nonetheless, and despite these divergences with regard to the nature and scope of non-interference, there does appear to be consensus regarding the indispensability of the non-interference requirement for any liberal freedom conception.

A second shared feature is less evident, and more difficult to specify. It concerns the connection between freedom and reason. In chapter 1 I argued that it is principally the thematization of this connection which sets the positive tradition apart from the negative one. It is also the principal ground of Berlin's repudiation of the former – largely on the grounds of his association of reason with truth. Yet, although the link between reason and truth may play a role in some proponents' accounts of positive freedom, for most it is the normativity of reason that is decisive. All freedom writers examined in this book, including Steiner, restrict freedom attributions to persons: all depart from Hobbes in this regard. All also attribute enormous normative significance to the idea of freedom – ironically perhaps, no one more so than Steiner, who nonetheless disavows a normative freedom approach. Their restriction of freedom attributions to persons strongly suggests that all of the theorists considered here think of persons as a class apart: as the only class of beings of whom freedom can be predicated. Once one inquires into the grounds of this restriction, references to persons' capacity for reason and to the normativity of reason usually follow – sometimes more, sometimes less obliquely. In Nozick we discovered a decisionistic model of practical rationality on the basis of which he accords persons status as setters of ends. In Steiner we eventually hit upon the idea of persons' capacity for incurring obligations as the normative ground of their equal right to negative freedom. Dworkin's responsibility principle presupposes persons' capacity for rational discrimination and judgement, and in Raz reasoning creatures are seen as uniquely responsive to normative aspects of the world. Each of the four contemporary liberal thinkers considered here reverts to persons' capacity for reason as a principal ground for freedom attribution at some point in his theory.

The puzzle is that, with the evident exception of Raz, the freedom-reason connection is not explored explicitly or at length by any of these writers. This failure is least surprising in the case of Steiner, who explicitly aims for a purely descriptive approach. It is most noticeable in Dworkin, whose freedom conception would be greatly enhanced, it seems to me, by the inclusion of a more sustained analysis of those aspects of moral personhood that justify, in Dworkin's view, the attribution to persons of quite such a demanding responsibility principle. In Dworkin, there is a *presumption* of a strong connection between practical rationality and the principles of ethical individualism, but little explicit exploration of that presumption. This omission contrasts with Raz's very clear delineation of the normativity of reason and its pervasive role in persons' perception of their social world. At the same time Raz's neo-Aristotelian conception is problematic in its own terms and at a considerable remove, moreover, from the modern problematization of the normativity of reason that is noticeable in the positive tradition – most acutely, perhaps, in Rousseau.

The attentive reader will have noted the relative failure of this book to find its way back to a more extended discussion of the freedom / reason connection, indicated in chapters 1 and 2, that characterizes the positive tradition: the Kantian notion, in particular, of freedom as a shared idea of reason the exercise of which presupposes the moral acknowledgement of its own rationally grounded constraints. In the Kantian idea of freedom – and arguably in that of the positive tradition more generally – the requirement of constraint by law is not extraneous to the idea of freedom as it is in the Hobbes-inspired negative tradition, where constraint by law is viewed as the very opposite of freedom as absence of constraint. Given the self-proclaimed Kantianism of much current mainstream liberal theorizing, I am somewhat surprised by this result. I had anticipated opportunities for a more sustained exploration of this aspect of the positive tradition in the context of contemporary freedom accounts, especially in the later chapters of this book. I found my inability to push either the chapter on Dworkin or that on Raz in that direction frustrating and disquieting at times. On reflection, however, the fact that current theorizing about liberal freedom often relies on *some* conceptual link between freedom and the normativity of reason which it nevertheless fails explicitly to thematize strikes me as an interesting conclusion in itself. When one considers possible reasons for this neglect, one ready answer may lie in Berlin's warning that the philosophical exploration of the freedom / reason connection issues all too easily in politically disastrous pronouncements about the truth of freedom and should, for that reason, be avoided. This warning reverberates with Berlin's metaphysics of human limitations – it is also suggestive of an unexpected underlying grasp on Berlin's part of the positive tradition's astute understanding of freedom as a morally and politically problematic modern idea. Again, the experience of human freedom as problematic is most acute in Rousseau, whose often extreme pronouncements are all too readily read out of context. In contemporary liberal freedom writings one rarely encounters either the positive tradition's philosophical unsettledness about freedom or Berlin's political anxieties about such philosophical unsettledness. Of the writers here considered, Raz seems to me to come closest to some such unsettledness – there is a dimension in

Raz's position suggestive of the thought that the idea of individual freedom needs to be socially contained if it is not to wreak havoc upon social living.

On the whole, however, contemporary theorizing about liberal freedom retains a stronger orientation towards the negative than the positive tradition. Even those whom I have decried as possessing positive leanings – certainly Dworkin – are probably best read as coming to that tradition through inflections of the kind proposed by Gerald MacCallum; that is to say, they tend to perceive the contribution of positive freedom as lying in the attention it draws to certain distributive requirements that arise in connection with the politics of freedom. Those aspects of the positive tradition seem to me to belong more to the Marxist and socialist appropriation of thinkers like Rousseau and Hegel – though the shift to social distributive concerns may form one indirect explanation of the relative neglect of the freedom / reason connection. A more direct explanation may lie in the broader philosophical tradition of contemporary Anglo-American liberal thinking which in the present context can be said to run from Hobbes and Locke to Hume and Mill, and which has always been more focused on the non-interference requirement, seeming, largely for that reason, more overtly political – at least if one understands by this a trained focus on the containment of coercive governmental powers. This contrasts with European philosophical culture – Rousseau and Kant, Hegel and Marx, including at least large aspects of Mill – in which the overall focus has been more on introspection and critique, whether of reason or of social conditions, and in which the idea of freedom has always had a correspondingly emancipatory yet nonetheless problematic character.

Considered from this perspective, Berlin's 'Two Concepts of Liberty' achieves its uniqueness, perhaps, through the way in which Berlin himself, standing between these two philosophical cultures, is able to relate them, albeit antagonistically, with one another, showing both to be aspects of a broader, shared liberal inheritance. Berlin understood very well that the positive freedom tradition does indeed form part of the liberal political and philosophical experience, despite his tendency to present the positive tradition as an aberration of liberal thought. And perhaps it is the case that, in the absence of the negative tradition as its counterweight, positive freedom, with its search for deeper moral meaning and more thoroughgoing political emancipation, more easily veers towards political disaster. But the same could be said of the negative freedom tradition, which without the need to bat back the tortured concerns of the positive tradition may run the contrasting danger of a market-oriented philistinism that confuses reason with choice and choice with freedom. Perhaps the best way in which to conceive of liberal freedom is not to think that one can subscribe to a version of either the negative or the positive variety. Perhaps divergent liberal freedom conceptions all occupy the space in between these two (not wholly accurate) historical poles, with some conceptions lying closer to one extreme than the other, but with all of them drawing inspiration, to varying degrees, from both sides.

Notes

Introduction: Approaching Liberal Freedom

1 Two very good introductions to the topic are Ted Honderich, *How Free Are You?* (Oxford: Oxford University Press, 1993), who defends a compatibilist position, and Robert Kane, *A Contemporary Introduction to Free Will* (Oxford: Oxford University Press, 2005), who argues in behalf of incompatibilism. For more demanding literature on this subject, see Gary Watson (ed.), *Free Will* (Oxford: Oxford University Press, 1982).

2 A very influential outline of the compatibilist / incompatibilist deadlock on this issue, and a compatibilist suggestion as to how to resolve it can be found in P. F. Strawson, 'Freedom and Resentment', in Watson (ed.), *Free Will*, 59–80.

Chapter 1 Isaiah Berlin: *Two* Concepts of Liberty?

1 All references to 'Two Concepts of Liberty' and to Berlin's related essays on freedom are to Isaiah Berlin, *Liberty*, ed. Henry Hardy (Oxford: Oxford University Press, 2002).

2 For an early response to Berlin's essay along these lines, see M. Cohen, 'Berlin and the Liberal Tradition', *Philosophical Quarterly* 10 (1960), 216–29. See also W. A. Parent, 'Some Recent Work on the Concept of Liberty', *American Philosophical Quarterly* 11 (1974), 149–67, and H. J. McCloskey, 'A Critique of the Ideals of Liberty', *Mind* 74 (1965), 483–508.

3 Examples include John Gray, *Berlin* (London: Harper Collins Publishers, 1995), and Michael Ignatieff, *Isaiah Berlin: A Life* (London: Chatto & Windus, 1998).

4 Gerald MacCallum, 'Negative and Positive Freedom', *Philosophical Review* 76 (1967), 312–34.

5 Unless otherwise indicated, I shall use 'freedom' and 'liberty' interchangeably in this and subsequent chapters.

6 Unsurprisingly, Berlin's thematization of value conflict within liberal theory has had an influence which has gone far beyond the freedom debate, raising the much broader question concerning value pluralism, and possible value conflict, as at the heart of the liberal creed. See John Gray, *Two Faces of Liberalism* (Cambridge: Polity, 2000).

7 Both these essays are reproduced in Berlin, *Liberty*, ed. Hardy.

8 Berlin, 'From Hope and Fear Set Free', in *Liberty*, 270.

9 Cf. Berlin, *Liberty*: 'Introduction', 4–10; 'Historical Inevitability', 122.

10 By 'conceptual sustainability' I mean to ask, in this context, whether a conception of freedom can be coherently formulated on the basis exclusively either of those aspects of the idea which Berlin associates with the 'negative' tradition, or on the basis of those he attributes to the 'positive' tradition. By 'substantive sustainability' I mean whether a conception of freedom that is formulated either in exclusively negative or in exclusively positive terms can offer an adequate understanding of freedom as a philosophical and moral idea.

11 Berlin, 'Two Concepts', 169.

12 Ibid.

13 This is not quite how Berlin himself puts it. According to Berlin, both types of liberal freedom invoke a 'non-interference' of sorts: however, while the negative tradition speaks of non-interference by *others*, the positive tradition invokes the idea of the non-interference of a person's irrational 'lower self' with their rational 'higher self' – a distinction which Berlin considers to be metaphysically nebulous and politically disastrous.

14 Berlin, 'Two Concepts', 172.

15 Ibid. 169.

16 For a clear and interestingly argued interpretation of Hobbes's philosophy, see Tom Sorell, *Hobbes* (London: Routledge, 1986). For good introductions to Hobbes's moral and political thinking, see Richard Tuck, 'Hobbes' Moral Philosophy', and Alan Ryan, 'Hobbes' Political Philosophy', both in T. Sorell (ed.), *The Cambridge Companion to Hobbes* (Cambridge: Cambridge University Press, 1996), 175–207 and 208–45 respectively.

17 Berlin, 'Two Concepts', 170.

18 Berlin's insistence that only other persons can render one unfree, and his attendant distinction between being unable and being unfree has contributed to the view of him as a libertarian in the political sense of the term, who rejects the idea that impersonal market forces and general social circumstances can render individual persons unfree. I believe that Berlin's position could be interpreted either way: in so far as the market / social circumstances are understood as deliberately constructed human arrangements, it may well be open to him to say that such humanly made structures can render particular individual agents unfree.

19 For a thorough and influential analysis of the concept of coercion, see Robert Nozick, 'Coercion', in P. Laslett, W. G. Runciman and Q. Skinner (eds.), *Philosophy, Politics, and Society*, 4th Series (Oxford: Blackwell, 1972), 101–35.

20 We shall return to the contrast between physical prevention and coercion in chapter 4 in the context of Steiner's descriptive theory of freedom.

21 Berlin, 'Two Concepts', 173.

22 Ibid. 172.

23 Ibid. 169.

24 Ibid. 178.

25 Kant is a difficult philosopher, and his theory of freedom is especially demanding and often misunderstood. For a very good general introduction to his philosophical system, see Otfried Höffe, *Immanuel Kant* (Albany, NY: SUNY Press, 1994). See also Roger Sullivan, *An Introduction to Kant's Ethics* (Cambridge: Cambridge University Press, 1994).

26 If Kant is difficult, many find Hegel even more demanding. For a very accessible introduction to Hegel's thought, see Peter Singer, *Hegel*, Past Masters Series, (Oxford: Oxford University Press, 1983). More demanding is Stephen Houlgate's excellent *An Introduction to Hegel: Freedom, Truth, and History* (Oxford: Blackwell Publishers, 2005).

27 Jean-Jacques Rousseau, *The Social Contract*, trans. G. D. H. Cole (London: Everyman, 1973). Good introductions to Rousseau include Robert Wokler, *Rousseau*, Past Masters series (Oxford: Oxford University Press, 1995); Chris Bertram, *Rousseau and the Social Contract* (London: Routledge, 2003). On liberty, see also Robert Wokler (ed.), *Rousseau and Liberty* (Manchester: Manchester University Press, 1995).

28 Rousseau, *Social Contract*, bk. 1, ch. 1, at 165.

29 On the difference between voluntaristic and intellectualist conceptions of reason and human willing in relation to human freedom, see Jerome Schneewind, *The Invention of Autonomy* (Cambridge: Cambridge University Press, 1998), 8–9. For a more

narrowly political approach to the same distinction see Patrich Riley, *Will and Political Legitimacy* (Cambridge, Mass.: Harvard University Press, 1982).
30 Berlin, 'Two Concepts', 179.
31 Ibid. 182.
32 Ibid. 190.
33 Ibid. 191.
34 See, e.g., S. I. Benn and W. L. Weinstein, 'Being Free to Act, and Being a Free Man', *Mind* 80 (1971), 194–211; W. Neely, 'Freedom and Desire', *Philosophical Review* 83 (1974), 32–54; G. W. Smith, 'Slavery, Contentment, and Social Freedom', *Philosophical Quarterly* 27 (1977), 236–48.
35 Again, Berlin's 'Introduction' is included in *Liberty*, ed. Hardy.
36 For a thorough discussion of the strength of this – possibly mistaken – intuition, see Smith, 'Slavery, Contentment, and Social Freedom'.
37 Especially relevant to this debate is Harry Frankfurt, 'Freedom of the Will and the Concept of the Person', in Watson (ed.), *Free Will*, 81–96.
38 Berlin, 'Introduction', 32.
39 Berlin, 'Hope and Fear', in *Liberty*, ed. Hardy, 273.
40 Berlin, 'Two Concepts', 173.
41 Berlin, 'Introduction', 5.

Chapter 2   Gerald MacCallum: Freedom as a Triadic Concept

1 One should, however, not overstate the effect of these biases on Berlin's philosophical argument.
2 For a well-known, terse statement and defence of logical positivism see A. J. Ayer's influential *Language, Truth, and Logic* (London: Pelican Books, 1971).
3 Ordinary language philosophy is primarily associated with the name of J. L. Austin. See his *How to Do Things with Words* (Oxford: Clarendon Press, 1962).
4 MacCallum's overall aims show some resemblance to Felix Oppenheim's earlier attempt to 'operationalize' the concept of freedom, thereby enabling its clear and non-ambivalent practical application. See Oppenheim's *Dimensions of Freedom: An Analysis* (New York: St Martin's Press, 1961). However, in contrast to MacCallum's purely conceptual approach, Oppenheim's is more empirical in orientation.
5 MacCallum, 'Negative and Positive Freedom', 314.

6 Ibid.

7 One might argue that Berlin can accommodate man-made socio-economic structures as potential sources of unfreedom, although this would have to involve a plausible case of showing that large-scale socio-economic structures are intentionally created or managed so as to curtail the freedom of some individuals.

8 Cf. John Gray, 'On Negative and Positive Freedom', in his *Liberalisms: Essays in Political Philosophy* (London: Routledge, 1989), 45–68.

9 MacCallum, 'Negative and Positive Freedom', 327–8.

10 Ibid. 316.

11 Ibid. 317.

12 Ian Carter suggests such a possible under-specification of the Z variable in his *A Measure of Freedom* (Oxford: Oxford University Press, 1999), 15–16.

13 See David Hume, *A Treatise of Human Nature*, ed. P. H. Nidditch (Oxford: Clarendon Press, 1978), p. III, sects 1–3. For an excellent general introduction to Hume's influential philosophy, including his conception of freedom, see Barry Stroud, *Hume* (London: Routledge, 1977). See also, more specifically, David Miller, *Hume's Political Thought* (Oxford: Oxford University Press, 1981), and J. L. Mackie, *Hume's Moral Theory* (London: Routledge, 1980).

14 Hume means by this phrase something very different from the commitment to an uncaused spontaneity of the will that I have ascribed to Berlin, and which has its modern philosophical source in Kant. Hume has in mind a kind of *caused* spontaneity: the will is free to choose between two options available to it, but the will's choice of one over the other is nonetheless explicable in causal terms. In order to avoid confusion, I shall henceforth distinguish between Humean caused spontaneity and Kantian uncaused spontaneity.

15 MacCallum, 'Negative and Positive Freedom', 320.

16 Indeed, we shall encounter it again, in a much more rigorously developed form than offered by Berlin, in chapter 3, when looking at Robert Nozick's libertarian defence of individual freedom.

17 For a contemporary restatement of the Kantian conception of reason and freedom as a shared capacity see Onora O'Neill, *Constructions of Reason* (Cambridge: Cambridge University Press, 1989). See, especially, Part I: 'Reason and Critique'. As we shall see in later chapters, especially chapters 5 and 6, it is noticeable that, despite the recent turn to 'Kantian liberalism', the connection between freedom and reason remains under-explored by those who claim broad allegiance to Kant's moral philosophy.

For the same reason, O'Neill's sustained philosophical and practical engagement with Kant's account of that connection places her in a critical relation with mainstream liberalism's underlying meta-ethical assumptions.

18 Although it must be conceded that this interpretative suggestion probably conflicts with Rousseau's overall voluntaristic conception of the will.

19 MacCallum, 'Negative and Positive Freedom', 325–6.

20 Ibid. 329.

21 Charles Taylor emphasizes this aspect of the positive tradition in his 'What's wrong with Negative Liberty?', in his *Philosophy and the Human Sciences* (Cambridge: Cambridge University Press, 1985), 211–30. See also his chapter entitled 'Atomism' in the same volume, (pp. 187–210).

Chapter 3   Robert Nozick: Freedom as a Property Right

1 Robert Nozick, *Anarchy, State, and Utopia* (Oxford: Blackwell Publishers, 1980), 169. For a clear and comprehensive introduction to Nozick's libertarianism, see Jonathan Wolff, *Robert Nozick: Property, Justice, and the Minimal State* (Cambridge: Polity, 1991).

2 Nozick, *ASU*, 150.

3 Thomas Nagel, 'Libertarianism without Foundations', in J. Paul (ed.), *Reading Nozick* (Oxford: Blackwell Publishers, 1982), 191–205.

4 One who similarly dissents from the majority view, though for different reasons, is Cheyney Ryan in his very helpful 'Yours, Mine, and Ours: Property Right and Individual Liberty', in Paul (ed.), *Reading Nozick*.

5 G. A. Cohen, *Self-Ownership, Freedom and Equality* (Cambridge: Cambridge University Press, 1995), 60–6. Like MacCallum, Cohen believes that it is possible to distinguish between 'moralised' and 'morally neutral' definitions of freedom, though Cohen's morally neutral definition differs from MacCallum's triadic definition in that Cohen seems to think that Y's non-interference with X's action is a sufficient condition of X's freedom.

6 Rights theorists generally distinguish between 'the will theory of rights' and 'the interest theory of rights'. The two types of rights theories start from very different meta-ethical assumptions regarding the normative grounds of rights. For a good discussion of the basic differences between them, see Matthew Kramer, John

Simmons and Hillel Steiner, *A Debate over Rights* (Oxford: Oxford University Press, 1998).

7 Cf. Nozick, 'Coercion'.

8 Cf. John Locke, *The Second Treatise of Government*, in *Two Treatises of Government*, ed. P. Laslett (Cambridge: Cambridge University Press, 1988), ch. 2. A careful introduction to Locke's philosophy can be found in John Dunn, *Locke*, Past Masters Series (Oxford: Oxford University Press, 1984). More demanding works on Locke's political philosophy include Richard Ashcroft, *Revolutionary Politics and Locke's Two Treatises of Government* (Princeton: Princeton University Press, 1986), and A. J. Simmons, *The Lockean Theory of Rights* (Princeton: Princeton University Press, 1992).

9 Nozick, *ASU*, 31.

10 Cf. Robert Nozick, 'Free Will', in his *Philosophical Explanations* (Cambridge, Mass.: Belknap Press, 1981), 291–361.

11 The obligation upon others not to treat persons in certain ways may give rise, indirectly, to persons' claims to specified domains of exclusive control; my point here is simply to say that on the relational view persons would not have a direct (natural) right, e.g., to private property.

12 Immanuel Kant, *Groundwork of the Metaphysics of Morals*, trans. H. J. Paton (New York: Harper Torch Books, 1964), 96.

13 Nozick, *ASU*, 49.

14 Ibid., emphasis added.

15 Ibid. 43.

16 Ibid. 50.

17 Nozick, *PE*, 291.

18 Ibid. 293.

19 See, on this, Robert Kane's masterful *The Significance of Free Will* (Oxford: Oxford University Press, 1996), ch. 7.

20 Nozick, *PE*, 295.

21 Ibid. 300.

22 Ibid. 304.

23 Ibid. 305.

24 Ibid. 306.

25 Ibid. 310.

26 Ibid. 312.

27 Nozick concedes that it may well not be non-question-begging. Michael Bratman concurs with Nozick's reservations in his 'Nozick on Free Will', in D. Schmidtz (ed.), *Robert Nozick* (Cambridge: Cambridge University Press, 2002), 155–74.

28 Serena Olsaretti, 'Freedom, Force, and Choice: Against the Rights-Based Definition of Voluntariness', *Journal of Political Philosophy* 6 (1998), 53–78, at 56.

29 Locke, *Second Treatise*, ch. 2, Sect. 6.
30 Cf. Berlin's distinction between 'being able to' and 'being free to' discussed in ch. 1.
31 Leif Wenar offers a nice counter-example to the complaint that Nozick's uses of the word 'freedom' are counterintuitive. Wenar suggests that, on the so-called non-moralized view of freedom as mere non-interference, we would have to hold that 'the exasperated mother of two screaming infants is free to hit the children with her shoe, or indeed to strangle them in their cribs'. Cf. Wenar, 'The Meanings of Freedom', in L. Thomas (ed.), *Contemporary Debates in Social Philosophy* (Oxford: Blackwell Publishers, 2007).
32 Cf. G. A. Cohen, *Self-Ownership, Freedom and Equality*, 60–7.
33 Leibniz's monadology has not itself directly to do with freedom: I use the term for analogical purposes.
34 Cf. Nozick, *ASU*, 174–5.
35 Cf. Locke, *Two Treatises of Government*, paras 36, 37.
36 Nozick's critics are united in their reaction (often of disbelief) to the logic of Nozick's distributive argument. See Onora, O'Neill, 'Nozick's Entitlements', in Paul (ed.), *Reading Nozick*, 305–22; Nagel, 'Libertarianism without Foundations'.
37 We shall encounter one prominent such view in chapter 5.

Chapter 4 Hillel Steiner: The Equal Natural Right to Pure Negative Liberty

1 This is not strictly speaking true: Nozick does allow the violation of individual rights in situations of extreme 'moral catastrophe'. Nonetheless, this sets the threshold considerably higher than non-libertarians would find morally reasonable or even plausible.
2 Other left-libertarians include Michael Otsuka, *Libertarianism without Inequality* (Oxford: Oxford University Press, 2003) and Philippe van Parijs, *Real Freedom for All* (New York: Oxford University Press, 1995). However, the 'pure negative freedom' conception is peculiar to Steiner's left-libertarianism.
3 The quantification, and hence measurability, of freedom is now a much-discussed topic especially among those who advocate freedom-based theories of distributive justice. Compare Carter, *A Measure of Freedom*; also, though from a very different perspective, Amartya Sen, *Development as Freedom* (New York: Knopf, 1999); and, more critically, Matthew Kramer, *The Quality of Freedom* (Oxford: Oxford University Press, 2003).

A discussion of these various approaches to the measurement of freedom is beyond the scope of this book, though it is worth pointing out that most of these recent attempts are inspired by Steiner's work.

4 Cf. Michael Otsuka, Hillel Steiner and Peter Vallentyne, 'Why Left-Libertarianism is neither incoherent, Indeterminate, or Irrelevant: A Reply to Fried', *Philosophy and Public Affairs* 33 (2005), 201–15.

5 There is a certain ambiguity in Steiner's contrast of his descriptive approach with what he calls 'evaluative freedom' conceptions. It is not clear whether by 'evaluative' Steiner has in mind normative freedom approaches more generally, or whether he regards evaluative accounts as a subcategory of the latter. Given his contrast of evaluative with descriptive approaches, I shall assume that by 'evaluative' Steiner means 'normative' in the broader sense. This tendency to conflate what Steiner describes as evaluative perspectives with normative approaches more generally seems to me mistaken: as we shall see below, Steiner has an excessively narrow understanding of evaluative-cum-normative freedom arguments. In the following I shall accordingly treat evaluative freedom accounts, as understood by Steiner, as a subcategory of normative freedom accounts more generally. More specifically, I shall keep to Steiner's denomination as 'evaluative' those freedom approaches which make essential reference to subjects' subjective mental attitudes – i.e. their desires, intentions, feelings, etc. By contrast, I shall speak of those approaches as 'normative' that include reference to persons' cognitive and practically rational capacities, including their capacity for moral respect, obligation, etc. I shall assume throughout that Steiner intends to keep his descriptive account free of reference both to evaluative attitudes and to normative capacities, and shall argue that he fails in this aim with regard to the latter.

6 I use the phrase 'world of reason' figuratively: I do not mean to imply that, for Kant, there are literally two distinct worlds. Although he has often been read in this way, I believe this to be mistaken. Compare P. F. Strawson, *The Bounds of Sense* (London: Methuen & Co., 1966), and Henry Allison, *Kant's Transcendental Idealism: An Interpretation and Defense* (New Haven: Yale University Press, 1983).

7 Recall here the distinctly Kantian flavour of Nozick's conception of rights as side constraints, as discussed in the previous chapter.

8 Hillel Steiner, *An Essay on Rights* (Oxford: Blackwell Publishers, 1994), 7.

9 Ibid. 8.

10 Ibid.

11 Ibid.
12 Cf. Steiner, *Essay on Rights*, pp. 22–32. Although Steiner offers an extended analysis and discussion of offers and threats and their lack of bearing on a person's pure negative freedom, his conclusion seems to me to be question-begging, in that, on a physicalist understanding of negative freedom, neither threats nor offers in any way affect how free a person is. Perhaps not, but rather than endorsing the conclusion, this may lead one to question the premiss.
13 Ibid. 33. Note here Steiner's apparent translation of Kant's formal freedom relation (a relation between the power of choice of one and that of another) into physicalist terms.
14 Ibid. 38–9.
15 Ibid. 37.
16 Ibid. 91.
17 See n. 3 above for relevant references.
18 For one such reading see Smith, 'Slavery, Contentment, and Social Freedom'.
19 Gray, *Liberalisms*, 54.
20 Ibid. 59.
21 Steiner, *Essay on Rights*, 17.
22 Ibid. 17–18.
23 For a thorough discussion of some of the computational problems involved, see Carter, *A Measure of Freedom*, ch. 7.
24 Kant, *Metaphysics of Morals*, 6. 231.
25 However, in *An Essay on Rights*, 39, Steiner does seem to endorse the Kantian conception of intelligible possession.
26 Ibid.
27 H. L. A. Hart 'Are There Any Natural Rights?', repr. in J. Waldron (ed.), *Theories of Rights* (Oxford: Oxford University Press, 1984), 77. In 'The Natural Right to Equal Freedom', *Mind* 133 (1974), 194–210, Steiner offers a detailed interpretation of Hart's position, which betrays considerable areas of substantive agreement between them.

Chapter 5 Ronald Dworkin: Liberty as an Aspect of Equality

1 In Ronald Dworkin, *Sovereign Virtue* (Cambridge, Mass.: Harvard University Press, 2002), 120.
2 By 'traditional libertarians' I here mean non-left-libertarians – although it should be added that left-libertarians' understanding of the (substantive) requirements of equal freedom nonetheless differs in important respects from that of Dworkin. Cf. chapter 4.

3 Cf. John Stuart Mill, *On Liberty*, ed. Gertrude Himmelfarb (London: Penguin Books, 1985). See esp. chapters 3 and 4. For a thorough and accessible introduction to Mill's philosophy, including his position on freedom, see John Skorupski, *John Stuart Mill* (London: Routledge, 1989).

4 It should be added that Mill and Dworkin additionally share a very strong suspicion of governments' tendency to abuse their coercive powers through unwarranted intrusions into individuals' private lives.

5 As we shall see in more detail below, the Millian understanding of personal autonomy is very different from Nozick's decisionistic account of individual self-creation.

6 Unfortunately, Dworkin nowhere elaborates on what precisely he means by an 'abstract ideal', nor where he thinks such come from.

7 Ronald Dworkin, 'Do Liberal Values Conflict?', in R. Dworkin, M. Lilla and R. B. Silvers (eds), *The Legacy of Isaiah Berlin* (New York: New York Review of Books, 2001), 73–90, at 83.

8 Ronald Dworkin, 'Do Liberty and Equality Conflict?', in P. Barker (ed.), *Living as Equals* (Oxford: Oxford University Press, 1996), 39–58, at 40.

9 Dworkin, *Sovereign Virtue*, 128.

10 Ibid. 162.

11 Quoted in John Hare, 'Kant on the Rational Instability of Atheism', in C. Firestone and S. Palmquist (eds), *Kant and the New Philosophy of Religion* (Bloomington: Indiana University Press, 2006), 60–85, at 75.

12 Dworkin, 'Do Liberty and Equality Conflict?', 42.

13 Ibid. 43.

14 Dworkin, *Sovereign Virtue*, 129.

15 Ibid. 133.

16 Ronald Dworkin, 'What is Equality I: Equality of Welfare', *Philosophy and Public Affairs* 10 (1981), 185–246, at 185.

17 Dworkin, *Sovereign Virtue*, 148.

18 John Rawls, *A Theory of Justice* (Oxford: Oxford University Press, 1973), 24.

19 The distinction is first introduced in Ronald Dworkin, 'What is Equality II: Equality of Resources', *Philosophy and Public Affairs* 10 (1981), 283–345.

20 There has been an enormous amount of literature published over the last twenty-five years on Dworkin's distributive theory. Much has focused on the distinction between option luck and brute luck. See esp. G. A. Cohen, 'Expensive Taste Rides Again', in J. Burley (ed.), *Dworkin and his Critics* (Oxford: Blackwell Publishing, 2004), 3–29; Michael Otsuka, 'Luck, Insurance, and Equality', *Ethics* 113 (2002), 40–54. A clear early critique can be found in

John G. Bennett, 'Ethics and Markets', *Philosophy and Public Affairs* 14 (1985), 189–204. See also Marc Fleurbaey, 'Equality among Responsible Individuals', in J. F. Laslier (ed.), *Freedom in Economics* (London: Routledge, 1998), 206–34, and Fleurbaey, 'Equality of Resources Revisited', *Ethics* 113 (2002), 82–105.

21 Samuel Scheffler, 'Choice, Circumstance, and the Value of Equality', *Politics, Philosophy and Economics* 4 (2005), 5–28, at 6.

22 Probably the most important critic from this perspective is Elizabeth Anderson, 'What is the Point of Equality?', *Ethics* 109 (1999), 287–337. But see also Scheffler, 'Choice, Circumstance, and the value of Equality', and Scheffler's excellent, 'What is Egalitarianism?', *Philosophy and Public Affairs* 31 (2003), 5–39.

23 On this last point see esp., Anderson, 'What's the Point of Equality?'.

24 Scheffler, 'Choice, Circumstance, and the value of Equality', 13. By 'libertarianism' Scheffler here means what I am calling 'incompatibilism'.

25 Ronald Dworkin, *Taking Rights Seriously* (London: Duckworth, 1977), 268.

26 Ibid. 258.

27 Ibid. 269.

28 Ian Carter, 'The Independent Value of Freedom', *Ethics* 105 (1995), 819–45. See also the extended discussion about kinds of value in relation to freedom in Carter, *A Measure of Freedom*, 31–67.

29 Scheffler, 'Choice, Circumstance and the value of Equality', 12.

30 Dworkin, *Sovereign Virtue*, 279.

31 Ibid. 250.

32 Ibid. 253.

33 Richard Arneson, 'Cracked Foundations of Liberal Equality', in Burley (ed.), *Dworkin and his Critics*, 79–98.

34 Dworkin, *Sovereign Virtue*, 242.

35 Ibid.

36 See, e.g., Will Kymlicka, *Contemporary Political Philosophy* (Oxford: Oxford University Press, 1991), ch. 3. More generally, see John Christman, 'Liberalism and Individual Positive Freedom', *Ethics* 101 (1991), 343–59; Paul Benson, 'Freedom and Value', *Journal of Philosophy* 84 (1987), 465–86.

Chapter 6 Joseph Raz: The Social Value of Personal Autonomy

1 For an overview of the idea of liberal neutrality see Robert E. Goodin and Andrew Reeves (eds), *Liberal Neutrality* (London:

Routledge, 1989). For an accessible outline of Raz's overall rela-
tionship to mainstream liberalism, see Stephen Mulhall and
Adam Swift, *Liberals and Communitarians* (Oxford: Blackwell
Publishers, 1992), ch. 8.

2 In this sense, both Nozick and Dworkin can be read as advocates
of versions of liberal neutrality – Nozick for negative, and
Dworkin for positive, reasons.

3 See esp., Joseph Raz, 'Facing Diversity: The Case of Epistemic
Abstinence', *Philosophy and Public Affairs* 19 (1990), 3–46.

4 By contrast, Rousseau does indeed speak of whole societies –
republics – being autonomous, and the contemporary idea of
national autonomy is much indebted to Rousseau's thoughts in
this regard.

5 Cf. Joseph Raz, *Practical Reason and Norms* (Oxford: Oxford
University Press, 1975), *idem, Engaging Reason* (Oxford: Oxford
University Press, 1999); *idem, The Practice of Value*, ed. R. J.
Wallace (Oxford: Oxford University Press, 2005).

6 Joseph Raz, *The Morality of Freedom* (Oxford: Oxford
University Press, 1988), 194.

7 Cf. Raz, *The Practice of Value*, 15–17.

8 Contrast this with Steiner's more Humean view of a close conceptual
relation between normativity and feeling. The association between
normativity and reason is shared by Aristotle and Kant, though they
give different accounts of that relation. In general, the contrasting
Humean contention that morality is a matter of feeling, rather than
either cognition or rational judgement, has held sway, at least until
recently, in modern Anglo-American moral and political thinking.

9 Raz, 'Explaining Normativity: Reason and the Will', in *Engaging
Reason*, 90–118, at 90.

10 Raz, 'Explaining Normativity: On Rationality and the
Justification of Reason', in *Engaging Reason*, 67–89, at 77.

11 Cf. Christine Korsgaard, 'The Dependence of Value on Humanity',
in Raz, *The Practice of Value*, 63–85.

12 Raz, *The Practice of Value*, 16.

13 Ibid.

14 Bernard Williams expresses perplexity over Raz's view, doubting
his ability sufficiently to differentiate it from value relativism, in
'Relativism, History, and the Conditions of Value', in Raz, *The
Practice of Value*, 106–20.

15 Raz, cited in Kramer, *The Quality of Freedom*, 155. Kramer dissents from Raz's view, favouring the method of conceptual analysis as outlined in chapter 2 of this book.

16 Raz, 16.

17 Nor, on the other hand, does he follow MacCallum in treating
them as constitutive components of the same concept of freedom.

18 Raz, 410.
19 Ibid. 409.
20 Ibid.
21 Ibid. 394.
22 Ibid. 369.
23 Ibid. 407.
24 Ibid. 423.
25 Ibid. 407.
26 Ibid. 370, n. 2.
27 See also Susan Wolf, 'Moral Saints', *Journal of Philosophy* 79 (1982), 419–39.
28 Raz, 369.
29 Ibid. 371. Raz's reference to 'coerced choices' signals his disagreement with someone like Steiner for whom, as we have seen, a person is free to do an action so long as they are not physically prevented from doing that action. A person who finds themselves confronted with the highwaymen's demand, 'Your money or your life', is confronted with a 'coercive choice'. On Steiner's account, such a person would be free, whereas in Raz's view they are denied the possibility of properly free, non-coercive choice.
30 Ibid.
31 Ibid. 390–1.
32 Ibid. 387.
33 A good representative example of what I call the mainstream choice-focused liberal position on the value of personal autonomy is Thomas Hurka, 'Why Value Autonomy?', *Social Theory and Practice* 13 (1987), 361–82. For a very useful and balanced overview of the liberal conception of autonomy in general, see Gerald Dworkin, *The Theory and Practice of Autonomy* (Cambridge: Cambridge University Press, 1988).
34 Raz, 375. It is questionable whether the ideal of self-realization as here defined by Raz is plausibly attainable by anyone. The demand that one realize *all* one's valuable capacities assumes that they are all compossibly realizable – a demand which strikes me as implausible.
35 But contrast Nozick's account of 'self-origination', examined in ch. 3 above.
36 Raz, 370.
37 Cf. ibid. 392.
38 Ibid.
39 Ibid. 385.
40 Ibid. 387.
41 A good example here might be parents who give up their careers to care full-time for their severely disabled children – children they might have chosen to have without bargaining for the

disability. Such parents act autonomously, on Raz's account, precisely in so far as they do accept that not everything in life is down to choice.

42 Raz, 155.

43 Note again that Raz's rejection of coercion as autonomy preventing is in line with Berlin and Nozick, and thus disagrees with Steiner's argument that coercion itself constitutes no freedom prevention.

44 Raz, 406.

45 Ibid. 378.

46 That said, Aristotle's own much-discussed ambivalence between the goodness of an active life compared to the goodness of the contemplative life might be interpreted as an early instance of Razian value incommensurability.

47 Raz, 404: 'Value pluralism not only admits the validity of distinct and incompatible moral virtues, but also of virtues which tend, given human nature, to encourage intolerance of other virtues.'

48 Ibid. 414.

49 Ibid. 380.

50 Ibid. 381.

51 Ibid.

52 Ibid. 394.

53 Ibid. 392.

54 For two different, insightful critical appraisals of the liberal overemphasis on choice, see Meir Dan-Cohen, 'Conceptions of Choice and Conceptions of Autonomy', *Ethics* 102 (1992), 221–43; also Claudia Mills, 'Choice and Circumstance', *Ethics* 109 (1998), 154–65.

55 An excellent general argument in favour of severing this tie is made by Dan-Cohen in 'Conceptions of Choice and Conceptions of Autonomy'.

56 Cf. Mills, 'Choice and Circumstance', 163–4.

Bibliography

Allison, Henry, *Kant's Transcendental Idealism: An Interpretation and Defense*. New Haven: Yale University Press, 1983.

Anderson, Elizabeth, 'What is the Point of Equality?', *Ethics* 109 (1999), 287–337.

Arneson, Richard, 'Cracked Foundations of Liberal Equality', in J. Burley (ed.), *Dworkin and his Critics* (Oxford: Blackwell Publishers, 2004), 79–98.

Ashcroft, Richard, *Revolutionary Politics in Locke's Two Treatises of Government*. Princeton: Princeton University Press, 1986.

Austin, J. L., *How to Do Things with Words*. Oxford: Clarendon Press, 1962.

Ayer, A. J., *Language, Truth, and Logic*. London: Pelican Books, 1971.

Benn, S. I. and W. L.Weinstein, 'Being Free to Act, and Being a Free Man', *Mind* 80 (1971), 194–211.

Bennett, J. G., 'Ethics and Markets', *Philosophy and Public Affairs* 14 (1985), 189–204.

Benson, Paul, 'Freedom and Value', *Journal of Philosophy* 84 (1987), 465–86.

Berlin, Isaiah, *Liberty*, ed. Henry Hardy. Oxford: Oxford University Press, 2002.

Bertram, Chris, *Rousseau and the Social Contract*. London: Routledge, 2003.

Bratman, Michael, 'Nozick on Free Will', in D. Schmidtz (ed.), *Robert Nozick* (Cambridge: Cambridge University Press, 2002), 155–74.

Carter, Ian, 'The Independent Value of Freedom', *Ethics* 105 (1995), 819–45.

Carter, Ian, *A Measure of Freedom*. Oxford: Oxford University Press, 1999.

Christman, John, 'Liberalism and Individual Positive Freedom', *Ethics* 101 (1991), 343–59.

Cohen, G. A., *Self-Ownership, Freedom and Equality*. Cambridge: Cambridge University Press, 1995.

Cohen, G. A., 'Expensive Taste Rides Again', in J. Burley (ed.), *Dworkin and his Critics* (Oxford: Blackwell Publishers, 2004), 3–29.

Cohen, Marshall, 'Berlin and the Liberal Tradition', *Philosophical Quarterly* 10 (1960), 216–29.

Dan-Cohen, Meir, 'Conceptions of Choice and Conceptions of Autonomy', *Ethics* 102 (1992), 221–43.

Dunn, John, *Locke*. Oxford: Oxford University Press, 1984.

Dworkin, Gerald, *The Theory and Practice of Autonomy*. Cambridge: Cambridge University Press, 1988.

Dworkin, Ronald, *Taking Rights Seriously*. London: Duckworth, 1977.

Dworkin, Ronald, 'What is Equality I: Equality of Welfare', *Philosophy and Public Affairs* 10 (1981), 185–246.

Dworkin, Ronald, 'What is Equality II: Equality of Resources', *Philosophy and Public Affairs* 10 (1981), 283–345.

Dworkin, Ronald, 'Do Liberty and Equality Conflict?', in P. Barker (ed.), *Living as Equals* (Oxford: Oxford University Press, 1996), 39–58.

Dworkin, Ronald, 'Do Liberal Values Conflict?', in R. Dworkin, M.Lilla and R. B. Silvers (eds), *The Legacy of Isaiah Berlin* (New York: New York Review of Books, 2001), 73–90.

Dworkin, Ronald, *Sovereign Virtue*. Cambridge, Mass.: Harvard University Press, 2002.

Fleurbaey, Marc, 'Equality among Responsible Individuals', in J. F. Laslier (ed.), *Freedom in Economics* (London: Routledge, 1998), 206–34.

Fleurbaey, Marc, 'Equality of Resources Revisited', *Ethics* 113 (2002), 82–105.

Frankfurt, Harry, 'Freedom of the Will and the Concept of the Person', in G. Watson (ed.), *Free Will* (Oxford: Oxford University Press, 1982), 96–110.

Goodin, Robert and Andrew Reever (eds), *Liberal Neutrality*. London: Routledge, 1989.

Gray, John, *Liberalisms: Essays in Political Philosophy*. London: Routledge, 1989.

Gray, John, *Berlin*. London: Harper Collins Publishers, 1995.

Gray, John, *Two Faces of Liberalism*. Cambridge: Polity, 2000.

Hare, John, 'Kant on the Rational Instability of Atheism', in C. Firestone and S. Palmguist (eds), *Kant and the New Philosophy of Religion* (Bloomington: Indiana University Press, 2006), 60–85.

Hart, H. L. H., 'Are There Any Natural Rights?', in J. Waldron (ed.), *Theories of Rights* (Oxford: Oxford University Press, 1984), 77–91.

Höffe, Otfried, *Immanuel Kant*. Albany, NY: SUNY Press, 1994.

Honderich, Ted, *How Free Are You? The Determinism Problem*. Oxford: Oxford University Press, 1993.

Houlgate, Stephen, *An Introduction to Hegel: Freedom, Truth, and History*. Oxford: Blackwell Publishers, 2005.

Hume, David, *A Treatise of Human Nature*, ed. P. H. Nidditch. Oxford: Clarendon Press, 1978.

Hurka, Thomas, 'Why Value Autonomy?', *Social Theory and Practice* 13 (1987), 361–82.

Ignatieff, Michael, *Isaiah Berlin: A Life*. London: Chatto & Windus, 1998.

Kane, Robert, *The Significance of Free Will*. Oxford: Oxford University Press, 1996.

Kane, Robert, *A Contemporary Introduction to Free Will*. Oxford: Oxford University Press, 2005.

Kant, Immanuel, *Groundwork of the Metaphysics of Morals*, trans. H. J. Paton. New York: Harper Torch Books, 1964.

Kant, Immanuel, *The Metaphysics of Morals*, trans. M. Gregor. Cambridge: Cambridge University Press, 1991.

Korsgaard, Christine, 'The Dependence of Value on Humanity', in J. Raz *The Practice of Value*, ed. R. J. Wallace (Oxford: Oxford University Press, 2005), 63–85.

Kramer, Matthew, *The Quality of Freedom*. Oxford: Oxford University Press, 2003.

Kramer, Matthew, John Simmons and Hillel Steiner, *A Debate over Rights*. Oxford: Oxford University Press, 1998.

Kymlicka, Will, *Contemporary Political Philosophy*. Oxford: Oxford University Press, 1991.

Locke, John, *Two Treatises of Government*, ed. P. Laslett. Cambridge: Cambridge University Press, 1988.

MacCallum, Gerald, 'Negative and Positive Freedom', *Philosophical Review* 76 (1967), 312–34.

Mackie, J. L., *Hume's Moral Theory*. London: Routledge, 1980.

McCloskey, H. J., 'A Critique of the Ideals of Liberty', *Mind* 74 (1965), 483–508.

Mill, John Stuart, *On Liberty*, ed. Gertrude Himmelfarb. London: Penguin Books, 1985.

Miller, David, *Hume's Political Thought*. Oxford: Oxford University Press, 1981.

Mills, Claudia, 'Choice and Circumstance', *Ethics* 109 (1998), 154–65.

Mulhall, Stephen and Adam Swift, *Liberals and Communitarians*. Oxford: Blackwell Publishers, 1992.

Nagel, Thomas, 'Libertarianism without Foundations', in J. Paul (ed.), *Reading Nozick* (Oxford: Blackwell Publishers, 1982), 191–205.

Neely, Wright, 'Freedom and Desire', *Philosophical Review* 83 (1974), 32–54.

Nozick, Robert, 'Coercion', in P. Laslett, W. G. Runciman and Q. Skinner (eds), *Philosophy, Politics, and Society*, 4th series, (Oxford: Blackwell, 1972), 101–35.

Nozick, Robert, *Anarchy, State, and Utopia.* Oxford: Blackwell Publishers, 1980.

Nozick, Robert, *Philosophical Explanations.* Cambridge, Mass.: Belknap Press, 1981.

Olsaretti, Serena, 'Freedom, Force, and Choice: Against the Rights-Based Definition of Voluntariness', *Journal of Political Philosophy* 6 (1998), 53–78.

O'Neill, Onora, *Constructions of Reason.* Cambridge: Cambridge University Press, 1989.

O'Neill, Onora, 'Nozick's Entitlements', in J. Paul (ed.), *Reading Nozick.* (Oxford: Blackwell Publishers, 1982), 305–22.

Oppenheim, Felix, *Dimensions of Freedom: An Analysis.* New York: St Martin's Press, 1961.

Otsuka, Michael, 'Luck, Insurance, and Equality', *Ethics* 113 (2002), 40–54.

Otsuka, Michael, *Libertarianism without Inequality.* Oxford: Oxford University Press, 2003.

Otsuka, Michael, Hillel Steiner and Peter Vallentyne, 'Why Left-Libertarianism is neither Incoherent, Indeterminate, or Irrelevant: A Reply to Fried', *Philosophy and Public Affairs* 33 (2005), 201–15.

Parent, W. A., 'Some Recent Work on the Concept of Liberty', *American Philosophical Quarterly* 11 (1974), 149–67.

Rawls, John, *A Theory of Justice.* Oxford: Oxford University Press, 1973.

Raz, Joseph, *Practical Reason and Norms.* Oxford: Oxford University Press, 1975.

Raz, Joseph, *The Morality of Freedom.* Oxford: Oxford University Press, 1988.

Raz, Joseph, 'Facing Diversity: The Case of Epistemic Abstinence', *Philosophy and Public Affairs* 19 (1990), 3–46.

Raz, Joseph, *Engaging Reason.* Oxford: Oxford University Press, 1999.

Raz, Joseph, *The Practice of Value*, ed. R. J. Wallace. Oxford: Oxford University Press, 2005.

Riley, Patrick, *Will and Political Legitimacy.* Cambridge, Mass.: Harvard University Press, 1982.

Rousseau, Jean-Jacques, *The Social Contract*, trans. G. D. H. Cole. London: Everyman, 1973.

Ryan, Alan, 'Hobbes' Political Philosophy', in T. Sorell (ed.), *The Cambridge Companion to Hobbes* (Cambridge: Cambridge University Press, 1996), 208–45.

Ryan, Cheyney, 'Yours, Mine, and Ours: Property Right and Individual Liberty', in J. Paul (ed.), *Reading Nozick* (Oxford: Blackwell Publishers, 1982), 323–43.

Scheffler, Samuel, 'What is Egalitarianism?', *Philosophy and Public Affairs* 31 (2003), 5–39.

Scheffler, Samuel, 'Choice, Circumstance, and the Value of Equality', *Politics, Philosophy and Economics* 4 (2005), 5–28.

Schneewind, Jerome, *The Invention of Autonomy*. Cambridge: Cambridge University Press, 1998.

Sen, Amartya, *Development as Freedom*. New York: Knopf, 1999.

Simmons, A. J., *The Lockean Theory of Rights*. Princeton: Princeton University Press, 1992.

Singer, Peter, *Hegel*. Oxford: Oxford University Press, 1983.

Skorupski, John, *John Stuart Mill*. London: Routledge, 1989.

Smith, G. W., 'Slavery, Contentment, and Social Freedom', *Philosophical Quarterly* 27 (1977), 236–48.

Sorell, Tom, *Hobbes*. London: Routledge, 1986.

Steiner, Hillel, 'The Natural Right to Equal Freedom', *Mind* 133 (1974), 194–210.

Steiner, Hillel, *An Essay on Rights*. Oxford: Blackwell Publishers, 1994.

Steiner, Hillel and Peter Vallentyne (eds), *Left-Libertarianism and Its Critics: The Contemporary Debate*. New York: Palgrave Publishers, 2000.

Strawson, P. F., *The Bounds of Sense*. London: Methuen & Co., 1966.

Strawson, P. F., 'Freedom and Resentment', in G. Watson (ed.), *Free Will* (Oxford: Oxford University Press, 1982), 59–80.

Stroud, Barry, *Hume*. London: Routledge, 1977.

Sullivan, Roger, *An Introduction to Kant's Ethics*. Cambridge: Cambridge University Press, 1994.

Taylor, Charles, *Philosophy and the Human Sciences*. Cambridge: Cambridge University Press, 1985.

Tuck, Richard, 'Hobbes' Moral Philosophy', in T. Sorell (ed.), *The Cambridge Companion to Hobbes* (Cambridge: Cambridge University Press, 1996), 175–207.

Van Parijs, Phillipe, *Real Freedom for All*. New York: Oxford University Press, 1995.

Watson, Gary (ed.), *Free Will*. Oxford: Oxford University Press, 1982.

Wenar, Leif, 'The Meanings of Freedom', in L. Thomas (ed.), *Contemporary Debates in Social Philosophy* (Oxford: Blackwell Publishers, forthcoming).

Williams, Bernard, 'Relativism, History, and the Conditions of Value', in J. Raz *The Practice of Value*, ed. R. J. Wallace (Oxford: Oxford University Press, 2005), 106–20.

Wokler, Robert, *Rousseau*. Oxford: Oxford University Press, 1995.

Wokler, Robert (ed.), *Rousseau and Liberty*. Manchester: Manchester University Press, 1995.

Wolf, Susan, 'Moral Saints', *Journal of Philosophy* 79 (1982), 419–39.

Wolff, Jonathan, *Robert Nozick: Property, Justice, and the Minimal State*. Cambridge: Polity, 1991.

Index